**New Directions for
Community Colleges**

Arthur M. Cohen
EDITOR-IN-CHIEF

Florence B. Brawer
Richard L. Wagoner
ASSOCIATE EDITORS

Carrie B. Kisker
Edward Francis Ryan
MANAGING EDITORS

Collaborations Across Educational Sectors

Marilyn J. Amey
EDITOR

Number 139 • Fall 2007
Jossey-Bass
San Francisco

COLLABORATIONS ACROSS EDUCATIONAL SECTORS
Marilyn J. Amey (ed.)
New Directions for Community Colleges, no. 139

Arthur M. Cohen, Editor-in-Chief
Florence B. Brawer, Richard L. Wagoner, Associate Editors

NEW DIRECTIONS FOR COMMUNITY COLLEGES (ISSN 0194-3081, electronic ISSN 1536-0733) is part of The Jossey-Bass Higher and Adult Education Series and is published quarterly by Wiley Subscription Services, Inc., A Wiley Company, at Jossey-Bass, 989 Market Street, San Francisco, California 94103-1741. Periodicals Postage Paid at San Francisco, California, and at additional mailing offices. POSTMASTER: Send address changes to New Directions for Community Colleges, Jossey-Bass, 989 Market Street, San Francisco, California 94103-1741.

SUBSCRIPTIONS cost $85.00 for individuals and $209.00 for institutions, agencies, and libraries in the United States. Prices subject to change. See order form at the back of book.

EDITORIAL CORRESPONDENCE should be sent to the Editor-in-Chief, Arthur M. Cohen, at the Graduate School of Education and Information Studies, University of California, Box 951521, Los Angeles, California 90095-1521. All manuscripts receive anonymous reviews by external referees.

New Directions for Community Colleges is indexed in CIJE: Current Index to Journals in Education (ERIC), Contents Pages in Education (T&F), Current Abstracts (EBSCO), Ed/Net (Simpson Communications), Education Index/Abstracts (H.W. Wilson), Educational Research Abstracts Online (T&F), ERIC Database (Education Resources Information Center), and Resources in Education (ERIC).

Microfilm copies of issues and articles are available in 16mm and 35mm, as well as microfiche in 105mm, through University Microfilms Inc., 300 North Zeeb Road, Ann Arbor, Michigan 48106-1346.

CONTENTS

EDITOR'S NOTES   1
Marilyn J. Amey

1. Demands for Partnership and Collaboration in Higher   5
Education: A Model
Marilyn J. Amey, Pamela L. Eddy, C. Casey Ozaki
This chapter describes a model that can serve as a lens for examining
community college partnership with a host of organizational collaborators, including the overall potential for achieving intended outcomes,
sustainability, and partner benefits.

PART ONE: Case Studies

2. Seamless Transition in the Twenty-First Century: Partnering   17
to Survive and Thrive
Gail Hoffman-Johnson
This chapter describes development and implementation of a strategic
partnership between a community college and a premier engineering
university to improve students' transition from the two-year to the four-
year institution.

3. Partnering to Move Students into College and Community-   29
Oriented Careers: The Administration of Justice Department at
East Los Angeles College
Carrie B. Kisker, Patrick Hauser
This chapter describes how the Administration of Justice Department
at East Los Angeles College has partnered with community and educa-
tional organizations to move students into college and careers in law
enforcement, criminal justice, and the fire service.

4. The Importance of Language, Context, and Communication   41
as Components of Successful Partnership
Susan J. Bracken
Successful community-university partnerships are usually attributed,
at least in part, to clear communication processes. This chapter reflects
on language and context as elements in developing a strong partnership
process.

5. Stepping Outside the Big Box High School: A Partnership   49
Influenced by Goals, Capital, and Decision Making
Jesse S. Watson
This chapter describes a partnership among a K–12 school district, a
community college, and a four-year university. It focuses on the role
that capital in various forms plays in the partnership.

PART TWO: Less-Than-Successful Experiences

6. Alliances Among Community Colleges: Odd Bedfellows or   59
Lasting Partners?
Pamela L. Eddy
This chapter discusses the experience of five two-year colleges that
formed a statewide alliance. It details how the motivation for joining
the alliance varied among the college leaders and describes the challenges the partners faced.

7. Lessons Learned from a Dual-Enrollment Partnership   69
Patricia L. Farrell, Kim Allan Seifert
This chapter presents lessons learned from a community college in Ari-
zona when implementing dual-enrollment partnership programs.

8. A Partnership in Flux: The Demise of a Program   79
Gay Garland Reed, Joanne E. Cooper, Llewellyn Young
This chapter explores issues surrounding the demise of a master's program, the Interdisciplinary Master in Education (IMED), that was delivered on the neighbor islands in the state of Hawai'i. The innovative
program brought educational opportunities to remote areas of the state
and was a partnership between the main campus in Honolulu and several community colleges.

PART THREE: Other Perspectives on Educational Partnership

9. The Legislative Playing Field: How Public Policy Influences   93
Collaboration
Debra D. Bragg, Maxine L. Russman
This chapter discusses collaboration associated with four public policies at the federal and state levels to show how partnerships are encouraged and how they struggle. The chapter concludes with lessons
learned about the complex intersection between policy and practice.

10. Strategies for the Future   105
C. Casey Ozaki, Marilyn J. Amey, Jesse S. Watson
This chapter revisits the partnerships described in this volume, using
the model outlined in Chapter One and introducing social and organizational capital as a largely ignored factor in the development and sustainability of partnerships.

INDEX   115

Editor's Notes

In response to myriad pressures to be more accountable and demonstrate educational outcomes, community colleges, public schools, and other institutions of higher education are searching for new ways to address student needs while responding to the demands of external entities. Community colleges in particular are challenged by accountability legislation, unstable state budgets, increased need and decreased funding for developmental education, rhetoric about seamless learning from kindergarten through college, high expectations from accrediting associations and grant makers, and the pressure resulting from operating in an ever-more-global society. Demands are high for innovative and alternative strategies that can meet educational standards and state needs while maintaining quality and access. It is not clear that our system—in which high schools, community colleges, four-year colleges and universities, and virtual universities operate in relative isolation from one another—will be able to effectively prepare students for jobs and careers in a knowledge economy.

To meet the learning needs of an increasingly diverse citizenry, and to face the economic, political, and accountability challenges just mentioned, education policy and decision makers are increasingly turning to partnerships. Across the nation, community colleges, K–12 school districts, and universities are collaborating with one another in creative ways that pool resources, increase access, and achieve numerous educational goals. Although not all partnerships include two-year colleges, these institutions serve as a bridge between public schools and four-year colleges, and between schools and the workforce. Community colleges naturally function as an intermediary among educational partners and are in a position to collaborate with an array of other institutions, among them for-profit educational service providers (for example, Sylvan Learning Centers), virtual universities, community organizations, and environmental agencies.

Advocates of collaboration between community colleges and other organizations—most often public schools and universities—argue that partnership results in a win-win situation that allows participants to obtain more results while using fewer resources. Traditional articulation and dual-enrollment agreements, for example, permit greater access to community colleges for many high school students and are considered to be beneficial to both community colleges and public schools. Despite the benefits in collaboration, many partnerships fail to obtain desired results, cannot be sustained, or cease to benefit both parties. In an era of increasing accountability, it is critical to understand why so many partnerships fall short of their goals,

New Directions for Community Colleges, no. 139, Fall 2007   © 2007 Wiley Periodicals, Inc.
Published online in Wiley InterScience (www.interscience.wiley.com) • DOI: 10.1002/cc.287

1

and to identify the factors that contribute to the success or failure of a collaboration. Highlighting important elements of educational collaboration, chapters in this volume offer a means to evaluate the effectiveness and efficiency of partnerships. They also look past the "value-added" rhetoric that accompanies most calls for educational alliances and more closely examine for whom a partnership is of value, at what cost, for what benefit, and the extent to which it is sustainable.

This volume of *New Directions for Community Colleges* should be helpful to those working with a community college partnership, especially college presidents, administrators, policy makers, faculty, public school and university leaders, and administrators with other educational provider organizations. State policy and decision makers involved with issues of educational access and accountability will also benefit from this volume, as will institutional researchers, who can gain from enhanced understanding of factors affecting the success and sustainability of community college partnerships, as well as those that contribute to perceived failure and termination. In addition, educators across institutional sectors who are interested in increasing access and addressing students' learning needs in a knowledge economy will learn strategies and shortcomings from the case examples given in this volume. Finally, university educators and researchers with an interest in community colleges will benefit from this important addition to the community college research base.

Chapter One, by Marilyn J. Amey, Pamela L. Eddy, and Casey Ozaki, describes a development model that can serve as a lens for examining partnerships. In Part One of the volume, chapter authors then present case studies of successful partnership and identify the keys to successful and sustainable collaboration. Gail Hoffman-Johnson presents the first of these case studies in Chapter Two, looking at development and implementation of a strategic partnership between a community college and a premier engineering university to improve students' transition from the two-year to the four-year institution. In Chapter Three, Carrie B. Kisker and Patrick Hauser discuss an innovative partnership between a college academic program and a local fire department. They analyze the factors that helped the collaboration succeed, including assessment practices, use of an advisory board, and the ability to leverage funding. Susan J. Bracken's Chapter Four examines the influence of language, context, and communication in successful partnership, presenting a case featuring a community college, a university, a government agency, and the community. Jesse S. Watson illustrates in Chapter Five the importance of champions and their ability to cultivate resources in a partnership among a community college, K–12 school district, and a university.

Part Two of the volume describes three less-successful or unsustainable partnerships, examines implications for college leaders, and suggests best practices for other strategic alliances. In Chapter Six, Pamela L. Eddy describes an alliance among five two-year colleges of technology in which partners were initially motivated to collaborate yet failed in the absence of factors that would contribute critically to sustainability. Patricia L. Farrell and Kim Allan Seifert's case looks at the challenges involved in creating a successful dual-enrollment program, even when state policy provides the structure to do so, in Chapter Seven. In the last chapter of Part Two, Gay Garland Reed, Joanne E. Cooper, and Llewellyn Young share their experience with a community college–university program partnership that began with great enthusiasm but, over a ten-year lifespan, became institutionally marginalized and eventually dissolved.

In Part Three, chapter authors examine educational partnership through other perspectives. Debra D. Bragg and Maxine I. Russman, in Chapter Nine, discuss collaboration associated with four public policies at the federal and state levels to show how partnerships are encouraged and how they struggle. The final chapter revisits the partnership model, drawing out themes and factors affecting successful collaborations that emerged in the preceding chapters. Recommendations for research and practice are also offered.

Marilyn J. Amey
Editor

MARILYN J. AMEY is professor and chair of the Department of Educational Administration at Michigan State University.

NEW DIRECTIONS FOR COMMUNITY COLLEGES • DOI: 10.1002/cc

1

This chapter describes a model that can serve as a lens for examining community college partnerships with a host of organizational collaborators, the overall potential for achieving intended outcomes, sustainability, and partner benefits.

Demands for Partnership and Collaboration in Higher Education: A Model

Marilyn J. Amey, Pamela L. Eddy, C. Casey Ozaki

Partnerships in academe are becoming more common, for a variety of reasons. Policymakers view partnership as a strategic way of meeting the state's education and economic goals. Institutions benefit from facilities and resource sharing (McCord, 2002; Sink, Jackson, Boham, and Shockley, 2004), and students gain access to additional instruction and a smoother transition to postsecondary education (Bragg, 2000). In addition, state governments are formulating policy to reward academic partnership, particularly those between K–12 schools and colleges. Sadly, although these partnerships are growing in popularity, relatively little is known about them. Of the research that exists, most is descriptive, focusing on a single institution or partnership. Of equal concern, most of the research highlights the K–12 institution and fails to discuss the perspective of the community college or four-year institution. To fill this gap in the literature and ultimately strengthen these partnerships, it is critical for policy makers and scholars to consider the process involved in establishing these arrangements, how they function, and the factors that help sustain them over time.

In this chapter, we discuss the elements and interactions involved in our partnership model. We begin by presenting the themes behind formation of a partnership, such as the reason for joining, the context of collaboration, process issues, and enhancing student learning. We then discuss the features of partnership, particularly the elements critical to initial development and

NEW DIRECTIONS FOR COMMUNITY COLLEGES, no. 139, Fall 2007 © 2007 Wiley Periodicals, Inc.
Published online in Wiley InterScience (www.interscience.wiley.com) • DOI: 10.1002/cc.288

early collaboration. We conclude by presenting some important questions to consider in evaluating collaboration or ongoing partnership. A visual depiction of the model highlights how the various aspects fit together.

Partnership Themes

Some researchers describe the community college as a broker, acting as a link between public schools and four-year colleges and often constituting the ideal intermediary among partnering units (Sink and Jackson, 2002). The college serves as an academic bridge for students and is often involved with a broad array of partners both within and outside the educational sector. As an entrepreneurial organization with a tradition of responsiveness, the institution serves as the link among public schools, businesses, and other governmental and community agencies. Finally, through use of distance learning, community colleges break down regional boundaries and expand our conception of and possibilities for partnership. However, in some of the literature on academic partnership the community college does not see itself in the role of broker. At times, it was the other partners that served in this capacity. This suggests the importance of determining, and not assuming, who or what provides the glue for a partnership in order to better understand the relationship and how it functions.

The literature also discusses several other themes that contribute to our understanding of institutional partnership. These themes broadly focus on the reasons for joining a partnership (Russell and Flynn, 2000), the context of a partnership (Watson, 2000), the process involved in sustaining a partnership (Fullan, 2002; Kotter and Cohen, 2002), and student learning issues (Chin, Bell, Munby, and Hutchinson, 2004).

Reasons for Joining. K–12 institutions and community colleges enter a partnership for a number of reasons (Russell and Flynn, 2000). Sharing facilities is one such impetus (McCord, 2002), stemming from the historic symbiotic relationship between these two levels of education in which early community colleges were an outgrowth of the K–12 system. Today, facility sharing is based on several strategic and economic factors. External pressures—resource scarcity, state mandates, and institutional goals—frequently constitute a compelling reason for a two-year college to work with other educational organizations. In this instance, partnering may be perceived as less voluntary than regulated or a matter of institutional survival. Technology demands (Sink, Jackson, Boham, and Shockley, 2004) also serve as a motivator for partners to pool scarce resources.

Personal relationships also serve as a reason for joining a partnership. Put another way, individuals from each institution may decide they have common interests that could be strengthened through a partnership. Such relationships may look more like Gray's definition of collaboration, a term often used synonymously with partnership. Gray (1989) views collaboration as the process by which parties who see the world differently search for solutions that go beyond their individual perspectives: "Collaboration transforms adversarial interaction into a mutual search for information and for solutions that allow all those participating to insure that their interests are represented" (p. 7). For example, in the case of developmental education, public school and community college leaders can collaborate to find a mutually beneficial response that serves the learning needs of their common community constituents. Collaboration implies interdependency and joint ownership of decisions. Although not always initiated in collegial fashion, Gray argues that collaboration involves problem setting, direction setting, and implementation, thereby amounting to a fairly logical approach to addressing organizational needs.

Defining the Context of Collaboration. To understand and assess partnership, one has to examine the context in which the partnership exists. Context typically involves internal and external organizational factors, sociopolitical climate, human resource concerns, and timing. The decision to partner takes place in a context, and that context shapes the decision and eventual development of any partnership. Because collaboration holds varying meanings for those involved (Watson, 2000), it is critical to develop a common understanding of relationships and roles involved in the partnership (Essex, 2001). These relationships span a continuum from formal to informal (Russell and Flynn, 2000), and their formality affects partnership stability and the extent to which relationships and roles need to be managed (Essex, 2001).

Consortia are a type of partnership that, though not always informal, are often perceived as voluntary and under member control. Baus and Ramsbottom (1999) describe the rise of educational consortia in the 1960s and 1970s to address common issues, primarily concerned with student needs. Often begun as voluntary collaboration, a consortium is multi-institutional and multifunctional and has long-term member support. Initial incentives to form a consortium typically revolve around academic issues such as cross-registration, faculty exchange, or use of other academic resources. Leadership at the highest level is typically required to make this form of partnership operate, especially if institutional policies and resources are centrally controlled. Clear role definition and communication of expectations are also required.

Process Issues. The literature also supports the idea that partnership is process-oriented and must be viewed as a living system (Morgan, 1998). Considering this, one sees it is critical to examine certain aspects of the partnership—such as who instigates the partnership, how members understand and interpret the relationships within the partnership, how the partnership changes over time, and how problems are resolved.

As with any other institutional endeavor, there is often a champion that pushes for and sustains the collaboration. The initiator can be an individual within the community college or a K–12 school, a member from the community, an employer, or students. Initiators bring with them forms and levels of power that are relevant to the partnership, notably reputation, resources, political influence, and expertise. The formal role of the initiator affects whether he or she has the power or authority to develop the partnership and sustain it over time. Moreover, the power bases are not evenly distributed or equally relevant to the partnership, so status differences may develop and cause relationship concerns.

Another process element is the development of the partnership itself. Even in a mandated arrangement, those involved participate in a kind of developmental process in their understanding of their roles, their work, and how they interact across organizational lines. To help explain this developmental process, Amey and Brown (2004) designed an interdisciplinary collaboration model that is based on a series of evolutionary stages. The model shows how members of a cross-organizational initiative (in this case, coming from departments) move from an individual orientation to a group orientation to a collaborative one. The Amey and Brown collaboration model shows that leadership shifts from being directive to facilitative, and then to inclusive and servant-oriented. As the partnership develops, aspects of it can be institutionalized. Establishing common language along with shared understanding as well as developing expectations, goals, and assessment measures represent movement toward making a partnership part of the life of the institutions involved.

Following on these more foundational aspects of sustainability, research on partnership development and organizational change emphasizes the need to make change stick (Kotter and Cohen, 2002). To institutionalize change efforts, the leaders must help others understand the link between the actions occurring and the desired outcomes (Fullan, 2002). Framing the partnership can result in multiple interpretation among partners, making sense of the situation for themselves (Eddy, 2003; Weick, 1995). Thus developing a shared meaning helps sustain the relationship.

Enhancing Student Learning. Many of today's K–14 educational partnerships are designed to strengthen student learning through high school achievement, college participation or degree attainment, or workplace preparation. Partnership is often developed to support cooperative work experiences that allow situated learning (Chin, Bell, Munby, and Hutchinson, 2004). Others focus on the transition for students from K–12 to higher education, from K–12 to work, and from community college to work (Bragg, 2000). Coupled with these initiatives is the concept of service learning that is frequently embedded in academic programming in schools and community colleges.

Partnership Model Development

Thus far, this chapter has focused on understanding the role of the two-year college as the entity responsible for drawing partners together. Despite perceived initial benefits, many partnerships fail to obtain desired results, cannot be sustained, or cease to benefit both parties. It is therefore also important to look past the rhetoric found with most calls for educational alliance and explore how these partnerships function. Highlighting important elements of educational collaborations is a way of evaluating their effectiveness and efficiency, and it can be accomplished by asking questions that examine their key components:

- What was the impetus to initiate the partnership? the reasons for joining? the antecedents (Gray, 1989; Russell and Flynn, 2000)? state, federal, or institutional policies?
- What is the context of the partnership? What are the economic, political, and sociocultural circumstances? What is the motivation for each partner to participate?
- How is the partnership understood by others, and what is the role of leadership in framing the partnership for constituents? How do the institutions involved and their members make sense of partnership (Watson, 2000)? Who is communicating with members about the partnership (Fullan, 2002)?
- What are the outcomes, benefits, and costs of the partnership? What kinds of assessment and benchmarking data about the partnership are gathered? Are goals and objectives revised appropriately? Do the data feed back into the partnership process (Kotter and Cohen, 2002)?
- What is required to sustain the partnership? If it is decided to continue the partnership, how will this be accomplished (Amey and Brown, 2004)? What resources are needed? How will they be garnered? If the partnership is to be dissolved or dramatically changed, who will manage this process and communicate it to others?

Using these questions as a foundation, we developed a multidimensional model based on the literature on K–20 partnerships as well as member checks with state community college representatives. The partnership model presents a fluid, interactive relationship. As we looked to better understand postsecondary partnerships and move beyond the descriptive narrative found in most of the literature, we used three frameworks to guide our thinking. Negotiated order theory (Strauss, 1978) informed our analysis of the origins of partnership, including who was involved, why, and to what ends. Sense-making theory (Weick, 1995) and framing (Eddy, 2003; Fairhurst and Sarr, 1996) presented ways to contextualize partnership and understand various perspectives that each player brought to the relationship. Finally, the framework of interdisciplinary collaboration (Amey and Brown, 2004; Creamer, 2003; Lattuca, 2001) allowed us to consider how partners might relate to and work with one another.

Partnership Development Process

Within the partnership development model (Figure 1.1), there are several components to consider: antecedents, motivation, context, and the partnership itself. Antecedents derived from the context and issues facing individual

Figure 1.1. Partnership Development Model.

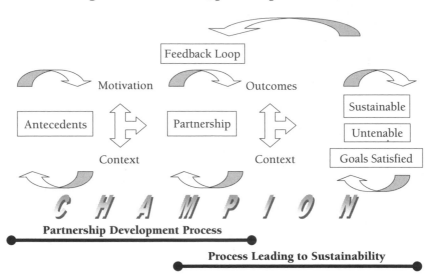

partners act as an incentive for the partnership. External policies or regulations, prior relationships, resource needs, or a challenging issue can all serve as an impetus. A precursor to successful collaboration involves developing shared understanding of the relationships and roles for all involved. These core relationships are on a continuum from very formal to informal. For example, colleges joined in partnership through an articulation agreement describe these relationships as very formal and probably do not think of them as collaboration so much as a form of cross-institutional contracts. At the other end of this continuum, a rural community college that opens its fitness facilities to local school teachers has an informal relationship that builds good will and the potential for more substantive collaboration in the future.

Motivation and its interplay with context are also important. As noted, reasons vary for institutions creating or joining a partnership (Russell and Flynn, 2000). The context of the initiative plays a critical role because the environment typically furnishes at least part of the rationale for initial involvement and usually has an impact on sustainability. State mandates, declining institutional enrollment or revenue, opportunities to share costs, grant funding initiatives, community needs, limited instructional capacity in certain subject matter, and unused facilities are just some examples of context that may stimulate the need for partnering. Within the motivation component of the model, partners may bring to the relationship varying levels of power or rationales for being involved. In part, the power that the partners bring comes from individual social capital (Coleman, 1988), which is grounded in the level of relational trustworthiness the individual engenders. The density of the relationship (Granovetter, 1983), which is based on the closeness of relationships, adds to the amount of power any one or more partners bring to the partnership. The champion in a partnership often has a high level of social capital to impart to the group. Another level of power emanates from organizational power or capital. Here, the partnering institutions and members have their own level of power to bring to bear within the group. Organizational capital emanates from control of resources or technology, information, and process (Morgan, 1998).

The fact that partners have their own reasons (motivations) for participating is not inherently problematic so long as the partnership is mutually beneficial. If benefits begin to accrue significantly more for one partner than another, motivation to participate can change. Those with less pressing or more tangential motivation tend to fall away from involvement in the partnership, become less active, or bow out altogether. Conversely, those with greater motivation to participate may overinvest without necessarily reaping comparable benefits. The key to the model, and partnership success, is how the institution and its members frame the partnership and how this changes as the partnership continues.

Once the partnership is established, it moves to the second stage of the model, which describes the long-term projections for the collaboration (sustainability, dissolution, failure, or completion of initial purpose). It is important to recognize that a partnership may end at any time in the process, before or after stated goals are accomplished, by mutual consent or without it. These ends may be positive and a natural finish (perhaps the objectives were fulfilled) or they may be "unnatural" (the project failed). It is also possible that individuals may leave the partnership for any reason. Although the partnership framework could still exist, the values, personalities, and working styles present at the onset may be altered considerably, thereby making the arrangement far less tenable or successful.

Two additional factors can be overlaid on this model to represent how partnership evolves: feedback and the champion. Within the early development and maintenance stages of partnership development, feedback is critical; it helps organizational members make sense of intended and actual outcomes. How the champion or organizational leaders frame the partnership is central throughout the process, and it also affects sustainability. Ongoing feedback is necessary and shapes decisions and contexts in all phases of the partnership, including whether to continue or dissolve the collaboration.

Another overarching factor in a partnership is the role of a champion. The champion is a person or group that advocates for the initiative. Typically, the champion believes in the partnership and its goals. The champion needs to have the support of the positional leader but does not have to be in a particular position of traditional power within the organization. This interpretation of the role differs from the change literature, which argues that the champion has to be in a formal leadership position. In a more inclusive approach to the champion role, the personal, cultural, and social capital that the champion maintains is often what contributes to success. At the same time, overreliance on a champion can detract from the institutionalization of the partnership. As with most features of academic organizations, those that continue over time become part of the culture and are built into administrative processes of the organization. This affords a greater degree of stability than the interpersonal dynamics associated with being too closely tied to a single individual within the organization.

Conclusion

Even though many believe that partnership is an effective strategy to meet K–16 educational demands, the reality is that this cross-organizational collaboration is often challenging to develop and hard to sustain. Having a conceptual model to analyze partnerships allows thinking more deeply and critically about the process of collaborating as well as constituting a means to determine if the partnership is successful. Institutional policy makers in turn can begin to look at a potential partnership by asking key questions of the partners.

Partnerships change and morph over time as issues change, the role of champion shifts, and new partners become involved. Sustainable partnerships are based on being flexible to new inputs and adjusting accordingly. If the partnership is seen as part of the organization's academic processes and therefore longer-term, new ways of conceptualizing and planning for the partnership need to occur, including considering how it will be sustained and institutionalized. If the collaboration is mandated or considered short-term, the developmental process is often ignored or short-changed and the partnership entails assumed rationale and buy-in. Such an arrangement is not often sustained; does not meet the objectives; or results in ill-will, misuse of resources, and organizational dysfunction. For viability over time, one must raise some additional questions that move beyond those accounted for in the conceptual partnership model:

- For how long in the process can differing motivations to partner coexist? How are motivations tied to institutional mission?
- How do you move past the champion role to institutionalizing the partnership? What is the role of the champion after the partnership has been institutionalized?
- How do you reconcile fundamental differences in organizational context?
- What happens if a critical person leaves the partnership?
- What is the impact of partner inequality on sustainability?
- Do differences in outcome for each partner affect sustainability?
- Is the partnership intended to be long-term or short-term?

The answers to these questions allow partners, policy makers, and constituents to think more fully about the goals of the partnership. Awareness of mental models underlying the motivation to participate in the group allows dialogue that creates shared meaning. Even the term *partner* may evoke contrasting meanings for those involved. Allowing for awareness of these elements of difference can lend support for the partnership so as to weather a period of contention or disagreement. Bringing the role of power differences to the surface aids acknowledgment early in the process. Policy makers in particular can use this model to better understand how to create a climate that promotes the type of partnership for which they are advocating.

References

Amey, M. J., and Brown, D. F. *Breaking Out of the Box: Interdisciplinary Collaboration and Faculty Work.* Boston: Information Age, 2004.

Baus, F., and Ramsbottom, C. A. "Starting and Sustaining a Consortium." In L. G. Dotolo and J. T. Strandness (eds.), *Best Practices in Higher Education Consortia: How Institutions Can Work Together.* New Directions for Higher Education, no. 106. San Francisco: Jossey-Bass, 1999.

Bragg, D. D. "Maximizing the Benefits of Tech-Prep Initiatives for High School Students." In J. C. Palmer (ed.), *How Community Colleges Can Create Productive Collaborations with Local Schools.* New Directions for Community Colleges, no. 111. San Francisco: Jossey-Bass, 2000.

Chin, P., Bell, K. S., Munby, H., and Hutchinson, N. L. "Epistemological Appropriation in One High School Student's Learning in Cooperative Education." *American Educational Research Journal,* 2004, *41*(2), 401–417.

Coleman, J. S. "Social Capital in the Creation of Human Capital." *American Journal of Sociology,* 1988, *94,* S95–S120.

Creamer, E. G. "Exploring the Link Between Inquiry Paradigm and the Process of Collaboration." *Review of Higher Education,* 2003, *26*(4), 447–465.

Eddy, P. L. "Sensemaking on Campus: How Community College Presidents Frame Change." *Community College Journal of Research and Practice,* 2003, *27*(6), 453–471.

Essex, N. L. "Effective School-College Partnerships: A Key to Educational Renewal and Instructional Improvement." *Education,* 2001, *121,* 732–736.

Fairhurst, G. T., and Sarr, R. A. *The Art of Framing: Managing the Language of Leadership.* San Francisco: Jossey-Bass, 1996.

Fullan, M. "The Change Leader." *Educational Leadership,* 2002, *59*(8), 16–20.

Granovetter, M. "The Strength of Weak Ties: A Network Theory Revisited." *Sociology Theory,* 1983, *1,* 201–233.

Gray, B. *Collaborating: Finding Common Ground for Multiparty Problems.* San Francisco: Jossey-Bass, 1989.

Kotter, J. P., and Cohen, D. S. *The Heart of Change: Real-Life Stories of How People Change Their Organizations.* Cambridge, Mass.: Harvard Business School Press, 2002.

Lattuca, L. *Creating Interdisciplinarity: Interdisciplinary Research and Teaching Among College and University Faculty.* Nashville, Tenn.: Vanderbilt University Press, 2001.

McCord, R. S. "Breaking the School District Boundaries: Collaboration and Cooperation for Success." *Education,* 2002, *123,* 386–389.

Morgan, G. *Images of Organization* (2nd ed.). Thousand Oaks, Calif.: Sage, 1998.

Russell, J. F., and Flynn, R. B. "Commonalities Across Effective Collaboratives." *Peabody Journal of Education,* 2000, *75*(3), 196–204.

Sink, D. W., and Jackson, K. L. "Successful Community College Campus-Based Partnerships." *Community College Journal of Research and Practice,* 2002, *26*(1), 35–46.

Sink, D. W., Jackson, K. L., Boham, K. A., and Shockley, D. "The Western North Carolina Technology Consortium: A Collaborative Approach to Bridging the Digital Divide." *Community College Journal of Research and Practice,* 2004, *28*(4), 321–329.

Strauss, A. *Negotiations: Varieties, Contexts, Processes, and Social Order*. San Francisco: Jossey-Bass, 1978.

Watson, L. W. "Working with Schools to Ease Student Transition to the Community College." In J. C. Palmer (ed.), *How Community Colleges Can Create Productive Collaborations with Local Schools*. New Directions for Community Colleges, no. 111. San Francisco: Jossey-Bass, 2000.

Weick, K. E. *Sensemaking in Organizations*. Thousand Oaks, Calif.: Sage, 1995.

MARILYN J. AMEY *is professor and chair of the Department of Educational Administration at Michigan State University.*

PAMELA L. EDDY *is associate professor in educational leadership at Central Michigan University.*

C. CASEY OZAKI *is a graduate research assistant in the Higher, Adult, and Lifelong Education Program in the College of Education at Michigan State University.*

NEW DIRECTIONS FOR COMMUNITY COLLEGES • DOI: 10.1002/cc

PART ONE

Case Studies

2

This chapter describes development and implementation of a strategic partnership between a community college and a premier engineering university to improve students' transition from the two-year to the four-year institution.

Seamless Transition in the Twenty-First Century: Partnering to Survive and Thrive

Gail Hoffman-Johnson

Only thirty years ago, colleges and universities struggled in isolation to meet the growing demand for postsecondary education. Twenty years ago, articulation agreements were the impetus for institutions to explore issues of access and quality with one another. Ten years ago, collaboration appeared on the higher education landscape. Operationalized in strategic partnerships, this trend shows no sign of abating in the early stages of the twenty-first century (Schaier-Peleg and Donovan, 1998).

Collaborative efforts appear to have great potential for increasing effectiveness and efficiency in the fiscally constrained environment of higher education. However, they represent a relatively new organizational arrangement about which we know very little. To better understand this new arrangement, it is helpful to consider the conditions that encourage collaboration within and between institutions. Understanding this emerging form of interinstitutional collaboration requires that we examine the forces that foster its development and facilitate or challenge its implementation. It is also critical to determine the appropriate outcomes, measures of success, and forces that lead to continued collaboration.

Recently, I had the opportunity to study a collaborative partnership between a public community college and a private, four-year university. In this case study, I found several factors led to the perceived success of this collaborative undertaking: a strong impetus for collaboration, the ability to

NEW DIRECTIONS FOR COMMUNITY COLLEGES, no. 139, Fall 2007 © 2007 Wiley Periodicals, Inc.
Published online in Wiley InterScience (www.interscience.wiley.com) • DOI: 10.1002/cc.289

create interdependence between the participating institutions, and an appreciation of the dynamic nature of these collaborative undertakings. Although these findings are congruent with prior research (Wilbur, 1996), they add important new dimensions to our understanding of collaboration. In particular, the need for a champion and the ability to foster a more collaborative attitude among faculty have implications for educational practice and policy.

In discussing this partnership, I present a multilayered story consisting of five parts. In the first two sections, I discuss the distinction between an alliance and a strategic partnership and describe the theoretical frameworks that guided this study. I then turn to the story of how the strategic partnership developed. Finally, I consider implications for both faculty and the institutions involved and conclude with recommendations.

Distinction Between an Alliance and a Strategic Partnership

Collaboration represents a relatively new response to the extraordinary challenges facing higher education in our resource-constrained environment. Conceptualization of collaboration varies widely, and there is little consensus on its core characteristics. Some view collaboration as focused, involving little more than cross-listing courses among institutions or joining two or more degree programs. To others, it entails new thinking, new forms of communication, and new structures. Certainly it is the latter perspective that is salient in the partnership highlighted in this chapter.

An *alliance* is far looser than a strategic partnership. In advocating strategic alliance as a response to the recent economic downturn, Martin and Samels (2002) defined it as a temporary, focused set of covenants between two or more complementary learning institutions or a learning institution and a business organization. Conversely, a *strategic partnership* is a legal relationship among parties having specified, joint rights and responsibilities as they work together to achieve common goals within an integrated whole. They are designed to develop an integrated educational structure to serve the needs of students, the institutions, area business and industry, and the surrounding communities (Martin and Samels, 2002). These partnerships are more encompassing than alliances because they foster healthy integration among several major sectors of society. As with any innovation, it is ambiguous and complex; the process of developing such a partnership is slow and fraught with challenges, especially in higher education.

Ways of Thinking About Partnerships

Several ways of thinking about partnerships are useful in understanding the situation I explored. I briefly explain them here so that the specific findings of my case are more clearly understood. Negotiated order theory (Fine,

1984) is a metaphorical way of looking at organizations that is concerned with examining how social structures are processed and how social processes become structured through negotiation (Basu, Dirsmith, and Gupta, 1999). Because I was interested in actors, tactics, and processes of negotiation, I used negotiated order theory to understand the development and implementation of this strategic partnership. Several elements of negotiated order are central to understanding partnerships. First, organization is impossible without some form of negotiation. Second, specific negotiations are contingent on organizational structure. Negotiation is patterned, not random, in that it follows lines of communication. Third, negotiation has a time limit; it is revised, renewed, and reconstituted as time passes. Fourth, structural changes in the organization require revision of the negotiated order; that is, the structure and internal politics of the organization are intertwined (Fine, 1984).

Building on these central tenets of negotiated order, Gray (1989) describes a process-oriented approach to creative problem solving in a turbulent environment. She observes that many issues seem unresolvable because our perception of how to function in an increasingly interconnected world is limited and suggests adopting a different approach to achieve creative solutions. Specifically, Gray encourages viewing problems from a number of perspectives and redesigning problem-solving strategies to include the various stakeholders who have an interest in the issue. She outlines a three-phase model of collaboration: problem setting, direction setting, and implementation. It is predicated on the assumption that a fundamental set of issues must be addressed during any collaboration and that some phases may take on more significance than others depending on the partnership.

In essence, Gray (1989) encourages reexamining how we organize to solve problems in contemporary society. Traditional models that stress independence are no longer suitable for managing in a turbulent world. Fundamental interdependencies are now necessary to institutional success, and a new metaphor is needed to help us understand what interdependence means. Gray suggests replacing the "pioneering" metaphor (rugged individualism in pursuit of one's own wants and desires) with a new vision emphasizing dynamic wholeness in which the parts of a whole are not distinct. Rather, individual parts derive their meaning in relation to other parts; change occurs as a reconfiguration of the entire set of relationships. Further, our present values and interactions, which emphasize independence, should be complemented with approaches that stress interdependence and mutualism.

To more fully understand what facilitates these new, cross-organizational designs, I turn to Kanter's model of innovation (1990). Kanter suggests that a dynamic model of innovation is necessary, connecting the major tasks of innovation—idea generation, coalition building, idea realization, and transfer or diffusion—to the structural arrangements and social patterns that foster them. Kanter argues that innovation is a set of tasks carried out by groups or individuals within the organization. These tasks are stimulated, facilitated, and enhanced—or deterred—by a set of macro-level conditions, often coming from outside the institution. Some of these structural and social factors are more important at certain stages and times than others. Kanter's model is particularly useful in looking at administrative innovation, which occurs when resources are scarce, and at process innovation, which occurs more often in established organizations. Considering that this case study involves established institutions that are attempting to do more than simply survive in a resource-constrained environment, both forms of innovation are important aspects of the partnership.

The Partnership Setting

Two Midwestern institutions developed and implemented a strategic partnership designed to customize education for students pursuing a baccalaureate degree. Although an articulation agreement had been in place for over a decade, campus leaders at Barone University and Vader Community College (both pseudonyms) sought to strengthen that relationship. The goal was to improve mechanisms for student support and thereby enhance access to careers in applied mathematics, applied physics, business, engineering, and environmental chemistry.

Hoping to expand the traditional articulation agreement into a more encompassing strategic partnership, senior administrators and an organizational consultant representing Barone University approached campus leaders at Vader Community College in 2002. University officials believed that formation of a strategic partnership with carefully selected community colleges could yield important benefits for several stakeholders. These benefits would accrue not only to the university but also to the participating community college, surrounding communities, employers, and students themselves. The fact that these two institutions voluntarily sought to partner is especially important considering that Barone is a four-year, private institution, whereas Vader is a two-year, public institution.

Recognizing the advantages of such an interorganizational arrangement for students and potential employers, the two institutions established an aggressive timeline, resulting in a signing ceremony for the strategic partnership less than a year after the problem-setting phase was initiated. At the ceremony, both college presidents spoke about the unique opportunities such a collaborative undertaking afforded. Considering that an articulation agreement alone can take far longer to complete, I assumed that there was incentive on both sides to bring the partnership to timely fruition. With this in mind, I chose to examine the nature of the two institutions to identify factors that played a role in developing and implementing this strategic partnership.

NEW DIRECTIONS FOR COMMUNITY COLLEGES • DOI: 10.1002/cc

The Partnership

Located in an economically ravaged city in the Midwest, Barone is an independent university specializing in closely coupled cooperative education at the baccalaureate level. It offers undergraduate programs in engineering, management, applied sciences, and mathematics, along with innovative graduate-level and continuing education programs. Barone's mission is to serve society by preparing technical and managerial leaders. Accredited in the early 1960s, Barone is considered one of the nation's premier cooperative institutions and is ranked as one of the country's top engineering institutions by *U.S. News and World Report*.

Vader, one of five community colleges with which Barone sought to partner, serves the same economically ravaged area. It too has been in existence for more than forty years and is accredited. Vader seeks to offer high-quality, accessible, and affordable educational opportunities and services and supports university transfer, technical, and lifelong learning programs.

Within this partnership, both Barone and Vader benefited. For example, Barone was able to refer interested students who were either academically underprepared or unable to afford the tuition to Vader, where they could receive special attention and support as they prepared for eventual transfer to Barone. Because Vader serves the same geographical area and is the largest single source of community college students to Barone, it made sense for the two institutions to work together.

Vader also benefited from the relationship. As with most community colleges, it is interested in successful transfer for its students to the university of their choice. However, because clear information about transfer is typically not available, it is difficult for the community college to facilitate the transition. Articulation agreements alone do not solve all of the problems community college students encounter when transferring. A strategic partnership between the university and the community college that includes careful, personalized advising as well as other forms of student support can address issues of academic as well as social integration in ensuring student success (Tinto, 1993) that go beyond the basics of an articulation agreement. Rather than being denied admission to Barone, Vader students are offered realistic alternatives to prepare for eventual admission, including advising into requisite science and math courses at the community college.

Local employers benefit as well. Advancing more students from the community college into the university's cooperative education programs in the emerging technologies of fuel cells, medical devices, and wireless capability was intended to help fill the gap created by the demise of the area's automobile manufacturing. Some employers, especially those with a shortage of engineers, may use this partnership to recruit local, talented students who desire to remain in the community and fill critical positions in their companies on graduation from Barone.

The Process of Partnering

To make the partnership a reality, the pair of institutions agreed to:

- Garner support from academic leaders at both schools. The college presidents, as well as other senior academic officers, student and educational support personnel, and faculty were involved in developing the partnership.
- Appoint a Barone liaison to work with a designated Vader staff person. Vader identified staff in admissions, articulation, and counseling and advising to work together with the Barone liaison to inform and support students interested in transfer to the university.
- Identify a Barone staff member and alumni to talk with students interested in transferring. A Barone admissions person spoke to Vader students in pre-engineering, upper-level mathematics, and physics classes. Barone regularly hosted open houses for interested students and their parents.
- Award scholarships. Barone is planning to award a scholarship to an outstanding community college graduate each year. An employer–community relations team was formed to explore opportunities related to this initiative.
- Sign a formal agreement outlining the strategic partnership. Vader and Barone signed a statement of partnership in May 2003; this document is subject to review every two years.

Throughout the entire process, John Bardy, an organization consultant hired by the university, acted as the driving force behind the entire collaboration. Bardy, who was highly respected by key university administrators, set about establishing an organizational link between Barone and Vader. The two presidents had previously agreed in concept to the partnership, so the official bridge between the two institutions was already in place. The presidents continued to supply necessary resources, primarily by empowering appropriate organizational members. A working group of key staff from both campuses met frequently under Bardy's direction and encouragement. Striving toward a common goal enabled this group to forge sound interpersonal relations. Staffing changes within the working group were kept to a minimum, ensuring continuity of personnel. In fact, nearly all of the same people were still involved two years later.

Addressing Faculty Resistance. Although a few key faculty members were involved from the beginning, most were initially resistant. Barone faculty had to be convinced that the institution's reputation as a premier engineering university would not be tarnished by aggressive pursuit of the transfer-student market. These faculty were accustomed to teaching students who were at the top of their high school class, and community college students represented an unknown quantity.

In addition to their initial resistance to teach transfer students, Barone faculty were also reluctant to examine community college courses for possible equivalency. It was no small feat to convince the faculty that such effort was indeed worthwhile. It was essential that faculty resistance to the university's plan to substantially increase the number of transfer students be overcome. Without their support, the strategic partnership was doomed. The Barone administrator in charge of college transfer partnerships summed it up this way: "One of the challenges sometimes is that the faculty get so entrenched in their particular discipline, and they're not willing to step beyond the bounds of their discipline border, boundaries. There aren't, in fact, many people, sadly, who look beyond their specific role or their unique institution. And I must admit, it's part of my learning curve coming out here."

One veteran faculty member at Barone, though, held a completely different view from his colleagues. Admittedly passionate about teaching chemistry and ensuring the viability of his program, he saw the partnership as a means to accomplish both. When asked what forces helped move the partnership along, this faculty member spoke about the desirability of having faculty from both institutions work together. Later in our conversation, when asked how effective he felt the partnership was in fulfilling its goals, he again mentioned the importance of having faculty work together.

The associate dean of science and math at Vader Community College proposed another important perspective: Barone must view Vader and its curriculum favorably. As she stated, "It is really important that Barone believes the quality of our courses is at the level that they need." She spoke of the involvement of key Vader faculty from physics, chemistry, and math in the early meetings, saying that these faculty "try to be ubiquitous for people that are developmental, they're thinking of all learning styles, and all previous math damage. But I think when you're competing in the big leagues and going to Barone, you do need academic challenge." Thus, although the Vader faculty were quite cognizant of the fact that they had to tailor their instruction to meet the diverse learning needs of their students, they also held "pretty high-end" expectations for those in the upper-level physics, chemistry, and math courses. By so doing, they ensured that Vader students would do well upon transfer to Barone.

A physical science instructor also lent a community college faculty voice. Relatively new to the Vader faculty, he was hired full-time during the fall of 2002, at a time when the partnership was being implemented. He soon became involved in reviewing and restructuring the engineering curriculum as well as advising students. He believed that one incentive for Vader to partner with Barone was to increase enrollment in the college's science and math courses, and to familiarize Vader students with the advantages of a Barone education. As he reported, "It really kind of fired people up about science and math, especially when they see Barone is ranked in the top ten in some of the different fields."

Empowering Staff and Celebrating Milestones. Another key aspect of this stage of innovation was procedural autonomy combined with multiple milestones. Although the presidents sanctioned the partnership, they stepped back to allow those with joint roles and responsibilities to work in creative isolation. A definite timeline was established for such key activities as planning meetings, open houses, and emerging technologies seminars. Milestones included a partnership signing celebration covered extensively by the local media and a reception held at the Barone president's home giving formal recognition to all the strategic partners.

Transfer and Diffusion. Even though I studied the partnership during its early stages, there was evidence of transfer and diffusion, Kanter's last phase of innovation (1990). Aspects of the partnership were embedding in ongoing organizational practice, and there was indication of some change within the organizations. For example, the presidents told me that the partnership was a frequent topic of conversation during their regular luncheons. In the beginning of the relationship, organizational members' roles and responsibilities were changed to ensure the success of the partnership, or at least to maximize potential for success. As the process evolved, fewer changes were needed. Barone was perceived as reaching out to Vader, creating organizational ties; most meetings took place on Vader's campus so as to be convenient to the community college administrators and faculty. Environmental receptivity was evidenced by the large number of interested transfer students and their parents at a recent Barone open house. Although extra chairs were brought in, several people still ended up standing throughout the hour-long session.

We have now seen how the environment created the need for a private, four-year engineering university to reconceptualize its perception of transfer students, primarily those at community colleges. This perceived need called for a new relationship between the university and the community college, a relationship characterized by shared goals and interdependence. In the process of working together, the strategic partnership emerged. The findings were consistent with existing theoretical frameworks (Gray, 1989; Kanter, 1990; Wilbur, 1996). However, certain aspects of the planning process were inconsistent with these theories. None of these frameworks accounted for the presence of a champion. In fact, the finding of a single sponsor, especially one outside of the presidency, is inconsistent with most of the change literature. Nonetheless, the importance and centrality of the champion in this partnership was clear and warrants further consideration.

The Role of the Champion. As an organizational consultant, Bardy was a champion who was influential in developing and implementing the strategic partnership. He acted much like a negotiator who knew how to approach the right people to get things done. He represented Barone but was simultaneously an outsider with many contacts in education, business, and industry. As a result, he was uniquely positioned to advance the partnership. Players at both Barone and Vader spoke very highly of him as an individual and his ability to plan, organize, and move the process along.

Implications

The initial question that stimulated my interest in looking at collaborative undertakings was "How does collaboration take place?" I was aware of the financial benefits of partnering but sought a more theoretical explanation, finding the work of Strauss (1978), Fine (1984), and Gray (1989) to be particularly informative. For example, I understood Bardy's role and work with the partnership through Strauss's properties influencing the negotiation context; the connections among negotiation, organizational structure, timing, and internal politics through Fine's conception of small- and large-scale negotiations in interorganizational relationships; and the various stages of the partnership evolution through Gray's process-oriented approach to negotiation.

Kanter's tasks of innovation were particularly helpful in understanding and overcoming faculty resistance in this strategic partnership. Broadly speaking, faculty represent the core of an educational institution, and they typically have great control over their own work. Power resides in their expertise; they have influence because of their knowledge and skills (Mintzberg, 2000). Accustomed to autonomy and academic freedom, faculty members tend to be internally focused. For these reasons, they often have a local (institutional) view rather than a more systemic one. Such a local orientation does not always fit with an institution that is engaging in partnership. Faculty are often less inclined to see the big picture that calls for new forms of organizational collaboration, new initiatives, and the need for innovation, especially if these changes affect them directly. For example, Barone faculty were not immediately willing to embrace the concept of increased transfer; they did not see value in working with the community college faculty to develop seamless transition for their students. At the same time, some faculty at both Barone and Vader adopted a more external focus and saw benefits accruing to students, the institutions, and the surrounding communities from involvement with the partnership. Part of the challenge for this partnership was to capitalize on structures and social connections that encouraged the latter view without disengaging those faculty who were initially resistant.

To meet this challenge, we must view colleges and universities as differing from other complex organizations. Their goals are less clear, they serve students rather than seek profit, and faculty dominate the decision-making process (Baldridge, Curtis, Ecker, and Riley, 2000). Having acquired considerable expertise in their field, faculty have been accorded autonomy in their work and freedom from supervision. As a result, they tend to be inwardly focused on their research, teaching, and service—attributes not conducive to the interdependence and mutualism required by the strategic partnership.

Several strategies were used to overcome this obstacle. Recall that the presidents of both institutions were committed from the outset to the partnership. They embraced the concept, shared it with their top administrators, and then stepped out of the way. It was the champion who subsequently capitalized on the structures and social connections necessary to create the interdependence that would make the partnership a reality. In large part, his effectiveness was due to relationships already in place, coupled with his ability to forge new ones.

As part of the partnership process, it was important to cross boundaries and build bridges. In doing so, increasingly frequent opportunities for communication about shared goals took place. By the very nature of their work, the presidents and top-level administrators held a cosmopolitan view. Issues of accountability, dwindling resources, and funding cuts were realities they could not ignore. Faculty, typically not concerned with such issues, became less resistant when encouraged to view these harsh realities from a systems perspective. A strong faculty voice from a respected colleague in conjunction with that of the administrators was a powerful force for needed change. In the end, it grew clear to the major players that the strategic partnership truly was an avenue designed to benefit students, the institutions, and the surrounding communities.

Recommendations

Faced with multiyear budget reductions that show no sign of abating and calls for increased accountability in higher education, collaboration offers a viable strategy for improving educational opportunities for all students. Regardless of the nature of the state-level higher education environment, this case study has implications for both policy makers and administrators trying to implement interorganizational collaboration. It highlights some of the issues, as well as the promise, of working together. On the basis of the strategic partnership studied, I make these recommendations:

- Offer incentives to encourage two- and four-year institutions to work together to create supportive educational environments to foster best practices in undergraduate education, including transfer systems
- Offer incentives to encourage institutional leaders at two- and four-year institutions to form strategic partnerships to eliminate duplication and redundancy of courses and programs
- Provide faculty with ongoing education and training to enable them to work collaboratively with those at their own institutions and at others
- Formulate institutional policies and educational practices that encourage faculty to invest more of their time and effort in working with colleagues at other two- and four-year institutions

One of the most important ingredients in any academic change effort is the increased external perspective of faculty (Wilbur, 1996). Once faculty make these external connections, they tend to be more receptive to new ideas, as well as more knowledgeable about how to implement them (Wilbur, 1996).

Although Barone faculty initially resisted, as time went on and the partnership took shape resistance dissipated.

Barone's initial strategy of simply awarding full tuition scholarships for increasing transfer student enrollment by itself did not solve the complex issues facing both institutions. In many ways, it exemplifies Gray's traditional pioneering metaphor, which is still all too common in higher education. On the other hand, creating a strategic partnership that encourages interdependence (Gray, 1989) involved incentives in addition to (or perhaps even in place of) the full tuition scholarship. This approach has a better chance of achieving the end goals and mutually benefiting both academic institutions.

Because they offer the possibility of greater interdependence, forms of collaboration offer much promise for addressing complex challenges such as transfer across quite distinct postsecondary institutions. The continued study of collaborative processes such as this strategic partnership increases our understanding of the issues and challenges stakeholders encounter in working together to accomplish a common goal.

References

Baldridge, J. V., Curtis, D. V., Ecker, G. P., and Riley, G. L. "Alternative Models of Governance in Higher Education." In M. C. Brown II (ed.), *Organization and Governance in Higher Education*. Boston: Pearson Custom, 2000.

Basu, O. N., Dirsmith, M. W., and Gupta, P. P. "The Coupling of the Symbolic and the Technical in an Institutionalized Context: The Negotiated Order of the GAO's Audit Reporting Process." *American Sociological Review*, 1999, 64(4), 406–526.

Fine, G. A. "Negotiated Orders and Organizational Cultures." *Annual Review of Sociology*, 1984, 10, 239–262.

Gray, B. *Collaborating: Finding Common Ground for Multiparty Problems*. San Francisco: Jossey-Bass, 1989.

Kanter, R. M. "When a Thousand Flowers Bloom: Structural, Collective, and Social Cognitions for Innovation in Organizations." In L. L. Cummings and B. B. Staw (eds.), *The Evolution and Adaptation of Organizations*. Greenwich, Conn.: JAI Press, 1990.

Martin, J., and Samels, J. E. "We Were Wrong: Try Partnerships, Not Mergers." *Chronicle of Higher Education*, 2002, 48(36), B10.

Mintzberg, H. "The Professional Bureaucracy." In M. C. Brown II (ed.), *Organization and Governance in Higher Education*. Boston: Pearson Custom, 2000.

Schaier-Peleg, B., and Donovan, R. A. "Building Local Partnerships: Contributions of a National Center." In D. McGrath (ed.), *Creating and Benefiting from Institutional Collaboration: Models for Success*. New Directions for Community Colleges, no. 103. San Francisco: Jossey-Bass, 1998.

Strauss, A. *Negotiations: Varieties, Contexts, Processes, and Social Order*. San Francisco: Jossey-Bass, 1978.

Tinto, V. *Leaving College: Rethinking the Causes and Cures of Student Attrition*. Chicago: University of Chicago Press, 1993.

Wilbur, S. "Understanding the Dynamics of Community College—University Collaboration: A Qualitative Study of a Transfer Admissions Program." Unpublished doctoral dissertation, University of California, Los Angeles, 1996.

GAIL HOFFMAN-JOHNSON is chair of the Business and Information Technology Division at Delta College in University Center, Michigan.

3

This chapter describes how the Administration of Justice Department at East Los Angeles College has partnered with community and educational organizations to move students into college and careers in law enforcement, criminal justice, and the fire service.

Partnering to Move Students into College and Community-Oriented Careers: The Administration of Justice Department at East Los Angeles College

Carrie B. Kisker, Patrick Hauser

In 1964, the American Association of Junior Colleges argued that "the two-year college offers unparalleled promise for expanding educational opportunity through the provision of comprehensive programs embracing job training as well as traditional liberal arts and general education" (p. 14). Community colleges hold unparalleled promise in part because of their close ties to private and public organizations in the local service area, their history of responding to community needs and demands, and their (literal and figurative) location between high school and four-year college or university. Indeed, the community college's ability to provide effective, hands-on job training is often dependent on partnership with other organizations. These relationships give students opportunities to gain a realistic understanding of what will be expected of them upon graduation, and they help create a seamless path from college to career. This is especially true in two-year college departments that prepare students for work in the community, as with law enforcement, criminal justice, and the fire service.

The Administration of Justice (AJ) Department at East Los Angeles College (ELAC) is no exception to this statement; its success in offering education and training rests in large part on its success in building and

maintaining numerous cross-sector collaborations. This chapter describes how the AJ department partners with high schools, four-year universities, local businesses, the fire service, law enforcement, and other public safety agencies to move students into college and community-oriented careers. We begin by illustrating the department's unique features and then describe four valuable practices that have allowed the AJ department to build and maintain strong partnerships and serve its students.

Description of ELAC's Administration of Justice Department

East Los Angeles College, located in Monterey Park, California (just east of downtown Los Angeles), is a comprehensive community college serving more than twenty thousand students each year (Los Angeles Community College District, 2006). The college's AJ department was created under the banner of police science shortly after establishment of the college to "lead the fight to prevent crime and injustice, enforce the law fairly and defend the rights of all, and partner with people we serve to secure and promote safety in our communities" (East Los Angeles College, n.d., n.p.). The AJ department, which presently includes criminal justice studies, a fire technology program, and an emergency medical technician (EMT) certification program, is one of the most popular occupational departments on campus; it enrolls nearly two thousand students each semester and saw a 400 percent increase in enrollment between 1999 and 2005. Departmental offices are located on ELAC's main campus, but many AJ and fire technology classes are offered at both the main campus and the college's South Gate Education Center (which educates a growing student population in the college's southernmost service area), as well as numerous other satellite locations.

Most departmental courses are offered both during the day and at night to accommodate students who are employed full-time or have other daytime commitments. As well, the AJ program at the South Gate Education Center offers several compressed courses. These courses, which are included in LEAP (the department's Law Enforcement Education Program), meet twice a week, carry either transfer or certificate credit, and compress a traditional sixteen-week term into eight weeks. South Gate's compressed courses are rotated every semester so that students can complete their entire program of study in the shortest possible time. ELAC's AJ department also offers courses during the summer months; in 2006, more than six hundred students enrolled in twenty course sections. The department has found that its summer classes helped to recruit (and in many cases, retain) students who were previously enrolled in AJ programs at other community colleges (East Los Angeles College, 2001).

Because the AJ department prepares students for careers in law enforcement, criminal justice, the fire service, and other community-oriented careers, partnership with community organizations, local high schools, and county and municipal agencies is critical to the department's ability to provide hands-on education and training, and to ensure that students transition into stimulating jobs on completion of the program. The department has partnered with the Los Angeles City Fire Department, the Los Angeles County Sheriff's Department, the Monterey Park Police Department, the Los Angeles County Probation Department, Catholic Big Brothers of Los Angeles, the East Los Angeles College Campus Sheriffs, and the Los Angeles County Community Development Commission; representatives from many of these organizations sit on the department's advisory committee. ELAC's AJ department also works closely with the college's psychology and sociology departments—as well as California State University, Los Angeles, and several local feeder high schools—to design academic programs and ensure course articulation. Later in this chapter, we discuss the importance of these partnerships in moving students into college and community-oriented careers.

Faculty. The AJ department at ELAC is staffed by six full-time faculty (including a department chair) and eighteen adjunct faculty, most of whom are current or retired public safety professionals. Faculty are active in various professional associations, including the California Association of Administration of Justice Educators, the California Community Colleges Association of Occupational Educators, the California Gang Investigators Association, the California Narcotics Investigators Association, the Association for Los Angeles Deputy Sheriffs, and the Los Angeles County Professional Peace Officers Association. Membership in these professional associations helps faculty stay current in their field and strengthens the department's network of professional relationships—a key factor in building and sustaining partnerships with public and community organizations.

Certificate and Degree Programs. East Los Angeles College's AJ department offers two associate degree programs, as well as seven certificate programs, five specialized course certificates, and a three-phase fire technology academy for high school students. The associate degree program in fire technology is designed for students preparing for a career in the fire service and for those who wish to transfer to a four-year university. Professional fire fighters supply hands-on training, and many courses are held at the Los Angeles County Fire Training Center, which allows students to observe the latest firefighting techniques. Recipients of ELAC's fire technology degree are qualified to enter the fire service, and two of the largest fire protection organizations in the area—the Los Angeles city and county fire departments—actively recruit graduates.

Similarly, ELAC's associate degree in administration of justice is designed for students who wish to transfer to a four-year university and those seeking employment in law enforcement and criminal justice. The program's advisory committee consists of professionals from county and municipal police and fire agencies, county probation and state parole offices, private security firms, and local EMT or ambulance companies. In addition, the committee includes representatives from local universities and certification agencies.

Advisory committee members are instrumental in helping students secure internships, as well as full-time employment on graduation. Both ELAC's fire technology and administration of justice majors are fully articulated with those at California State University, Los Angeles, and course numbers and content have been updated to ensure consistency with classes offered at other Los Angeles community colleges and local four-year universities.

In addition to its two associate degree programs, ELAC's AJ department offers seven certificate programs. The Administration of Justice, General Studies certificate is designed for students seeking entry-level employment in criminal justice and private security agencies and is awarded to students on completion of eighteen units (six selected courses) in the AJ major. The fifteen-credit Administration of Justice, Law Emphasis certificate is designed for students seeking a broad, law-based perspective in administration of justice studies and prepares them for administrative and law-based employment in the criminal justice field. The Administration of Justice, Sociological Emphasis certificate was developed in conjunction with ELAC's sociology department and requires students to complete nine units (three classes) in the AJ department as well as six units in the sociology department. Completion of this certificate program gives students a basic knowledge about the sociological aspects of crime (including the social causes of crime and delinquent behavior) and prepares them for entry-level positions in probation, parole, corrections, and law enforcement.

ELAC's AJ and psychology departments jointly offer the Chemical Dependency Specialist in Criminal Justice certificate program. This fifteen-unit course sequence consists of two classes in the AJ department and three psychology courses; it prepares students for entry-level positions in assessment and treatment of incarcerated substance abusers. In many cases, completion of this certificate is a precursor to students going on to complete the state-certified, thirty-one-unit chemical dependency counseling certificate offered by the Psychology Department. The AJ department also offers a Forensic Crime Scene Analyst certificate, developed with significant input from members of the Los Angeles County Sheriff's Department's Scientific Services Detail as well as other current industry professionals. The certificate is a sequence of six classes (seventeen units) that prepares students for employment as a crime scene technician, evidence custodian, or coroner's assistant and includes a field observation or internship component.

The fire technology program within the administration of justice department offers an Emergency Medical Technician (EMT) certificate, as well as EMT recertification courses. Currently, the vast majority of fire service agencies require possession of an EMT certificate as a prerequisite for employment. The program also offers a Fire Technology certificate, composed of five core courses (fifteen units) in the discipline. These core courses are articulated with the California State University, Los Angeles Fire Technology Department and prepare students for entry-level employment with the fire service.

In addition to these more traditional certificate programs, ELAC's AJ department also offers several one-course skills set certificates. In many cases, these courses are similar to the basic instruction recruits receive at the Los Angeles Sheriff's Training Academy, and on completion of each course students receive certificates from both the sheriff's department and the college. These skills set certificates are especially advantageous for those who are currently employed in law enforcement and who wish to be promoted or gain training points. Another single-course certificate, Fingerprint Classification and Identification, is required by the City and County of Los Angeles for an applicant to sit for the entry-level qualification examination for employment as a fingerprint identification technician.

Although high school dual-enrollment students are welcome to enroll in AJ courses so long as they have parental and high school consent, the department also offers a program specifically for high school students interested in fire technology. The FIRE (Fire Instruction, Recruitment, and Education) Academy is sponsored by ELAC and the Los Angeles City Fire Department and enrolls students from three local high schools. Named an outstanding collaboration with business and industry by the Los Angeles Community College District, this four-year-old partnership brings together two-year college faculty and seasoned fire technology professionals to hold seven-week courses in which high school students learn the basics of the fire industry, leadership skills, and workplace practices and ethics. As a local Monterey Park newspaper reported, the FIRE program not only recruits students to East Los Angeles College and the fire service but also "provides them with positive role models who will encourage them to continue to strive towards their academic and career goals" ("ELAC's F.I.R.E. Academy . . . ," 2002).

Students. The student body in the AJ department is diverse in terms of ethnicity and gender. Despite the fact that the criminal justice and fire technology fields have historically been considered male occupations, nearly two-thirds of students are female. Indeed, the department makes a concerted effort to recruit females and bilingual Latinos and ensures that these students have role models and mentors in the faculty and among its partner organizations. Departmental recruitment and mentoring efforts seem to be working; in response to a 2004 survey about their experiences in the FIRE Academy, all ten female students surveyed strongly agreed with the statement "I feel that the academy would encourage other girls that may not think they could succeed in a career with the fire service" (East Los Angeles College, 2004).

Students are recruited into ELAC's AJ department in several ways. In addition to the proactive recruitment measures undertaken by the college's outreach and recruitment office, the department has an articulation agreement with Roosevelt High School, which ensures a seamless transition from high school to college, and participates in recruitment visits to other feeder high schools. The department also collaborates with the Los Angeles County Sheriff's Explorer Academy, which enrolls high school students in courses offered at ELAC's main campus, South Gate Education Center, the Sheriff's

Department training center, as well as local sheriff's stations. Students earn college credit for completing the Explorer Academy and receive encouragement, motivation, mentoring, supervision, and counseling from sheriff's deputies and department faculty. Many of the students who complete the Explorer Academy go on to matriculate at ELAC's AJ department. In addition, AJ maintains a close collaborative relationship with ELAC's tech prep department, a program that encourages high school students to use a career ladder of courses and related experiences for a more seamless transition from high school to career and technical education.

Administration of Justice Students Club. A unique feature of the department is its AJ Students Club, a voluntary, student-centered extracurricular activity that reinforces concepts learned in traditional courses, helps students apply theory to practice, and offers them opportunities to look behind the scenes of the criminal justice system. The club was created to address common misperceptions about the criminal justice profession, and to create opportunities to interact with and mentor students outside of the traditional classroom environment. More than one hundred students are members of the AJ Students Club, twenty-five of whom attend the South Gate Education Center. Additionally, thirty of the student club members attend classes in the evenings, and some are high school dual-enrollment students.

The club gives its members practical exposure to their field of study through field trips to police training centers, prisons, and other community organizations; guest speakers; and on-campus demonstrations by police agencies. Departmental partnerships with the Sheriff's Training Academy, the Sheriff's Weapons Training Center and Special Enforcement Bureau, and the Los Angeles Police Department's training center have also created opportunities for students to participate in role-playing exercises. Collaborative relationships between the AJ Students Club and numerous community organizations have also led to internship programs for club members.

A vitally important aspect of the AJ Students Club is its focus on service to the community. This focus helps students connect with one another, with law enforcement professionals, and with the communities they will be working in; it reinforces concepts such as diversity, tolerance, cooperation, and respect within the criminal justice field. For the last three years, the club has sponsored Thanksgiving food drives and Christmas toy drives, both of which have substantially benefited numerous deserving local families. This focus has also led to creation of a scholarship program for AJ students who are continuing their education at ELAC or in criminal justice programs at four-year universities. Between 2000 and 2006, the AJ Students Club has raised and awarded more than $20,000 in scholarship funds for deserving students. In addition, Melinda Vasquez, a 2001 program graduate, started her own nonprofit organization and funds one of the annual scholarship awards, earmarked for a single Latina mother aspiring to employment within the criminal justice system.

NEW DIRECTIONS FOR COMMUNITY COLLEGES • DOI: 10.1002/cc

Awards. The AJ department at East Los Angeles College has been recognized at both the local and state levels for its innovative preservice and inservice training programs for criminal justice and fire technology personnel. It has also won several Excellence in Workforce Development awards from the Los Angeles Community College District and the California Community College Association of Occupational Educators. As mentioned earlier in this chapter, the FIRE Academy was dubbed an outstanding collaboration with business and industry by the Los Angeles Community College District in 2005. Much of the department's success can be credited to its unique relationships with criminal justice agencies, including the Los Angeles County Sheriff's Department, as well as a dedicated advisory committee that continually strives to create relevant and engaging learning experiences for students.

Best Practices in Partnering to Move Students into College and Community-Oriented Careers

East Los Angeles College's AJ department relies extensively on partnerships with public agencies, community organizations, high schools, and four-year universities to deliver relevant education and training that can successfully and seamlessly move students into college and careers. The next sections describe four valuable practices that have allowed ELAC's AJ department to build and maintain strong partnerships and effectively serve its students.

Collaboratively Identify Departmental Mission and Culture. As Kisker and Carducci (2003) note, establishing a shared mission among all partners in an educational collaboration is critical to the program's success. ELAC's AJ department has worked closely with faculty, staff, students, and community partners to collaboratively identify the department's mission and vision. Not only has this process resulted in a comprehensive mission statement but it has enabled the department to build and maintain the community partnerships necessary to ensure that students can move seamlessly from high school to college and into careers. The AJ department's stated mission is as follows: "The Administration of Justice Department at East Los Angeles College is committed to the academic and professional success of its students. We are dedicated to nurturing their personal growth, character development, and individuality. It is our mission to assist every student in reaching his or her fullest potential" (East Los Angeles College, n.d., n.p.). The mission statement then goes on to list seven ways in which the department carries out its mission, one of which discusses the importance of partnership.

In developing this mission statement, department leaders sought input from faculty, students, staff, and community partners as they recognized that buy-in from all of these groups would be necessary. In particular, faculty must commit to continuing their own professional and academic development to ensure that their students receive the most current and informed instruction, and representatives from community organizations must commit to mentoring students and make available internship opportunities and

NEW DIRECTIONS FOR COMMUNITY COLLEGES • DOI: 10.1002/cc

other activities that engage students in their learning and help them move seamlessly into a career. By creating a mission statement that is detailed enough to define stakeholder responsibilities yet broad and flexible enough to evolve over time, the AJ department publicizes its goals and expectations and creates a compact with students and community partners.

Establish a Diverse Array of Community Partners. Community-oriented programs such as those offered in ELAC's AJ department cannot effectively move students into college and career without a diverse array of partners who are committed to the same goals. Indeed, the department's partnerships with all sectors of its service group—including feeder high schools, local businesses, public agencies, other departments on campus, and four-year universities—are a key factor in the department's success. These partnerships allow the department to recruit secondary students into its programs and ensure a seamless transition from high school to college, offer joint certificate programs with ELAC's psychology and sociology departments, and send a great many students on to a criminal justice or fire technology major at a four-year university. They also ensure that students receive excellent instruction and mentoring, hands-on training, and realistic expectations about careers in law enforcement, criminal justice, and the fire service.

For example, in partnership with the Los Angeles County Sheriff's Department the AJ department offers a Sheriff's Affiliated Training and Education Program, which allows sheriff's personnel to earn academic credit for in-service training courses at ELAC. This program offers both long-term and short-term courses that were collaboratively developed by AJ staff members and representatives from the sheriff's department and approved by campus and district curriculum committees. The FIRE Academy is another example of a program that would not be possible without the extensive involvement of a community partner. The program places participants on a path toward employment with a fire agency, spurs high school students' interest in postsecondary education, and builds self-esteem.

Perhaps one of the most important ways in which the AJ department involves community partners in student learning is by asking them to sit on a departmental advisory committee. As Kisker and Carducci (2003) have pointed out, establishing a shared governance structure, such as an advisory board made up of community and private-sector representatives, is an effective strategy for ensuring that a program's shared mission and goals remain at the center of all programmatic and instructional decisions. ELAC's AJ advisory board consists of representatives from several high-profile law enforcement agencies and faculty from other local universities and community colleges in the district. Advisory committee members have input into the items and recommendations discussed at the annual advisory committee meeting. The diversity of adviser perspectives ensures that the AJ department considers new courses and activities from a broad range of perspectives, and that it continuously thinks about how to improve student learning and create new professional opportunities. The department regu-

NEW DIRECTIONS FOR COMMUNITY COLLEGES • DOI: 10.1002/cc

larly communicates with its advisory board, and distributes a biannual newsletter with news about the department, upcoming programs and activities, and discussion of how community partners can continue to support the department and its students.

Treat Students as Partners in Their Learning. As important as it is to build and maintain meaningful relationships with representatives from the community, it is also vital to treat students as partners in their learning. Faculty and staff in ELAC's AJ department view students as consumers whose repeat business and loyalty must be earned. Staff members personally follow up with every single student referred by ELAC's Tech Prep coordinators, and instructors frequently survey students about their experience in departmental programs and activities as well as modify coursework and instruction as appropriate.

Departmental faculty members are also explicit about their expectations for students. Student performance expectations are passed out at the beginning of every course, and faculty hold students to a high level of academic performance. For many entering students, especially those from low-performing high schools, ELAC's AJ department is the first place they encounter instructors who communicate a belief in their ability. Though such high expectations are often stressful, students know that faculty, staff, and community partners are there to help them along the way; the department firmly believes in and practices the notion that "students don't care how much you know until they know how much you care."

Furthermore, the department furnishes students with the resources they need to succeed in their courses and careers: mentoring, tutoring, resumé development, one-on-one meetings with faculty, and so forth. The department makes all of these resources available, but it is up to students to take advantage of them; from orientation through commencement, faculty and staff communicate to students that they are responsible for their own learning and success. Treating students in this way—as partners—encourages them to think constructively about their future and what they need to do to accomplish their goals. Community and business partners are essential to reinforcing the student-as-partner concept; they model the behaviors and characteristics that are vital to workplace success and expect students to do the same.

Leverage Resources. A significant challenge facing community college partnerships with business and community organizations is linked to the relative instability of funding for collaborative programs, especially in times of scarce financial resources (Kisker and Carducci, 2003). To combat this challenge, ELAC's AJ department has worked hard to leverage Perkins, Tech Prep, and vocational and technical education (VTEA) funding from the California Community Colleges chancellor's office to obtain extra resources. The FIRE Academy is a successful example of how ELAC's AJ department has leveraged VTEA funds to support collaborative educational programs.

For example, there are specific required uses for VTEA funds, which may not be used to supplement existing programs. Some of the required uses are offering students strong experience in all aspects of an industry; initiating, improving, expanding, and modernizing quality vocational and technical education programs; and linking secondary and postsecondary vocational and technical programs (Los Angeles Community College District, 2007). The FIRE Academy successfully meets these required uses.

Similarly, although ELAC's AJ department provides most of the funds necessary to operate the Sheriff's Affiliated Training and Education Program, the Sheriff's Department recently sold a fully equipped police vehicle to the department for one dollar. Instructors use the vehicle—which is adorned with custom graphics and "ELAC AJ Dept." insignia—to teach police tactics, and it is also used to assist in recruitment and outreach at feeder high schools. A fully equipped ambulance used in EMT training was obtained from PRN Ambulance, a local ambulance company. PRN and numerous other local ambulance companies actively recruit ELAC graduates for EMT positions; a recent program graduate reported that fifteen of sixteen members of his ambulance company's shift were graduates of ELAC's EMT training program.

In addition, in 2006 the AJ department received a $50,000 grant from the California Governor's Office of Homeland Security to improve its ability to effectively respond to a catastrophic incident; at the time the grant was received, ELAC was the only community college in the state to receive such funding. The AJ department's revised response plan, recommendations, and other fruits of the grant are intended to ultimately establish a best-practices model for how community colleges and other educational institutions can effectively respond to a critical incident.

Conclusion

As we noted at the start of this chapter, the success of many community college departments—especially those that offer hands-on occupational training or prepare students for careers in the community—depends on how well the department builds and maintains collaborative relationships with public and private organizations. The Administration of Justice Department at East Los Angeles College has been highly successful in establishing partnerships with local community and educational partners. All parties have benefited greatly: students who may not have considered college to be an option have matriculated at ELAC and gone on to four-year universities or careers that allow them to serve their community; faculty and staff gain instructional partners and the ability to give students stimulating, hands-on training; and the local sheriff's department, fire department, probation office, and other community partners gain a steady stream of knowledgeable workers who can hit the ground running.

In many ways, ELAC's AJ department exemplifies the American Association of Junior College's vision (1964) that community colleges offer "unparalleled promise for expanding educational opportunity"; its partnerships with high schools and four-year universities ensure a seamless path from secondary to postsecondary education, and its collaborative relationships with community agencies offer students stimulating, realistic education and training as well as clearly defined paths to a career in law enforcement, criminal justice, or the fire service. Although each community college has unique characteristics, goals, and circumstances, the best practices described in this chapter constitute a useful blueprint for creating and maintaining cross-sector collaborations that effectively move students into college and community-oriented careers.

References

American Association of Junior Colleges. *A National Resource for Occupational Education.* Washington, D.C.: American Association of Junior Colleges, 1964.

East Los Angeles College, Administration of Justice Department. "A.J. Department Bits and Pieces." *Scales of Justice,* Oct. 2001, p. 2.

East Los Angeles College, Administration of Justice Department. *F.I.R.E. Academies Student Survey Analysis.* Monterey Park, Calif.: East Los Angeles College, 2004.

East Los Angeles College. *Advisory Committee Handbook.* Monterey Park, Calif.: East Los Angeles College, 2006.

East Los Angeles College, Administration of Justice Department. *Our Mission.* Monterey Park, Calif.: East Los Angeles College, n.d.

"ELAC's F.I.R.E. Academy Preps Future Fire Fighters." *Monterey Park Cascades,* July 1, 2002, p. 11.

Kisker, C. B., and Carducci, R. "Community College Partnerships with the Private Sector—Organizational Contexts and Models for Successful Collaboration." *Community College Review,* 2003, *31*(3), 55–74.

Los Angeles Community College District. *Fast Facts.* Los Angeles: Los Angeles Community College District, 2006 (http://www.laccd.edu/about_us/fast_facts.htm; accessed May 25, 2007).

Los Angeles Community College District. *Workforce Development. VTEA: Vocational and Technical Education Act. Use of Funds.* Los Angeles: Los Angeles Community College District, 2007 (http://www.laccd.edu/workforce_dev/vtea/use-of-funds.htm; accessed May 25, 2007).

CARRIE B. KISKER is an educational consultant for Santa Monica College and the California Community College Collaborative at the University of California, Riverside.

PATRICK HAUSER is chair of the Administration of Justice Department at East Los Angeles College in Monterey Park, California.

NEW DIRECTIONS FOR COMMUNITY COLLEGES • DOI: 10.1002/cc

4

Successful community-university partnerships are usually attributed, at least in part, to clear communication processes. This chapter reflects on language and context as elements in developing a strong partnership process.

The Importance of Language, Context, and Communication as Components of Successful Partnership

Susan J. Bracken

Educational partnership is complex and challenging, and a significant amount of literature is devoted to understanding the reasons some partnerships are successful and others—even with good people and good ideas—fail. In a review of the literature, Tett (2005) found that successful partnerships are clear about the purpose of their endeavor, and that members reach agreement about who is responsible for which aspects of the partnership. A good partnership recognizes that each member's unique contributions reflect trust and commitment to clear communication. This is demonstrated by a "commitment to learning from each other and changing our own ideas as a result" (Tett, 2005, p. 6). In the opposite light, Tett, Crowther, and O'Hara (2003) argue that barriers to successful partnerships stem from differences in funding, perceived power, purpose, organization culture, ideology, processes, and communication styles. Further, they suggest that lack of flexibility, accommodation, or resources, or inability to deal with conflict, will potentially lead to failure.

This chapter analyzes the role language, communication, and context play in a successful collaboration among several community colleges, a university, a government agency, and a number of communities. The examples in this case focus on the early phases or stages of partnership formation as discussed by Amey and Brown (2005).

NEW DIRECTIONS FOR COMMUNITY COLLEGES, no. 139, Fall 2007 © 2007 Wiley Periodicals, Inc.
Published online in Wiley InterScience (www.interscience.wiley.com) • DOI: 10.1002/cc.291

Exploring the Case: What Happened?

In 2004, I evaluated a partnership planning process with a twofold purpose. First, the partnership sought to increase the interest level of K–12 students and their parents in careers in science, math, and technology. In addition, the project wanted to increase the public's general appreciation of the contributions that science, math, and technology make to our everyday lives. The overall plan was to begin working in one or two pilot states and subsequently develop a model that could be expanded nationally. The partners included community college and university faculty, administrators, staff, and students; government agency educational directors, staff, and researchers; and community volunteers, teachers, parents, and nonprofit administrators. Later in the process, several small groups of high school students were included. Huxham and Vangen (2000) would describe the partners' purpose as seeking a collaborative advantage, in which the groups could accomplish more collectively than individually. In my role as an evaluator, I observed and participated in phone conferences with representatives from each group and observed planning meetings and a multiday planning workshop. I also collected survey data, conducted several focus groups, and shared my observations and analysis with the planning group.

Initially, there was considerable synergy; the planning group members were enthusiastic about working together and took steps to learn about one another. During this period, everyone seemed to agree that they shared an educational outreach philosophy: grassroots involvement through mutual collaboration. In the initial conversations, representatives from the community college (the partnership developers), a government agency, and a university made it clear that they had limited financial resources to share. The local community and nonprofit members stated that they understood acquiring joint funding would be necessary. At first, I was surprised with the level of agreement and how quickly the planning group reached consensus. It was also surprising that the use of similar or even identical language seemed to be facilitating the process.

After the initial meetings, small conflicts and tensions began to surface. The conflicts appeared to be submerged or masked by differences in communication and context hidden beneath similar language. In other words, because the planning group members were using similar language, they assumed they understood one another and therefore ignored small warning signs about differing perspectives or ideas that needed to be clarified.

Huxham and Vangen (2000) discuss partnership in terms of our membership in various groups. They theorize that group membership needs to be examined and its complexities and dynamics explored through analysis of language as reflective of our organizational, professional, ethnic, and cultural lenses. In the case of this multisector partnership, commonalities in language temporarily obscured differences in context and communication.

NEW DIRECTIONS FOR COMMUNITY COLLEGES • DOI: 10.1002/cc

By developing and applying a strategy of language and context awareness, the groups were able to successfully move forward.

Grassroots Involvement Through Mutual Collaboration

When the government agency, university, and community college group members initiated the project, they approached it as they would their other projects. They invited colleagues who they felt had expert knowledge in science, math, or technology, or who were known for their productivity. As part of the formation process, the partnership conveners (the community college, university, and government agency) put forward their most knowledgeable members. The conveners also wanted the group to act as a grassroots organization, so they worked to recruit local community members. However, because obtaining access to the local community proved difficult, the organizing partner agencies invited several community and nonprofit groups to participate as a strategy to recruit local community members. This invitation proved problematic because the original conveners saw the community agencies simply as a tool to recruit additional participants, whereas the community agencies expected to play a more substantial role within the organization. This construct is discussed in detail by Tett (2005) as the distinction between *involvement* and *empowerment*. The community college, university, and government partners wanted to involve the community members. The community members, using the same collaborative language as the postsecondary and government members, had their own understanding and were acting and expecting to act as fully empowered members.

This difference in understanding manifested itself in several skirmishes and power struggles. For instance, the community members invited several high school students to participate in the process, thinking it was a natural way to develop age-appropriate strategies and information. However, the government and postsecondary partners were confused by the addition of members who they felt had little or no expertise to offer. In turn, the community members dug in their heels and insisted that the best way to reach the community was to include representatives of the target audience. In large part, this conflict developed because the group members did not communicate with one another. Huxham and Vangen (2000) discuss the concept of group membership and stress that selection of partners plays a role in the hidden communication process. Assessment of which groups a member belongs to, as well as the member's status and degree of responsibility, is a critical element in the communication subtext.

In the end, the high school students stayed and appeared to be willing to ignore the undercurrents by participating enthusiastically in the planning process. They expected to be fully participating members and to be seen as experts on their own age group and interests. In the end, the collective

NEW DIRECTIONS FOR COMMUNITY COLLEGES • DOI: 10.1002/cc

group began to joke about differences in language, vocabulary, and experience and began to listen more attentively to one another's thoughts.

Resources as an Issue: "We Do Not Have Any Money!"

In my observation, this phrase emerged early in the first conference call and was repeated in every phone call and meeting that took place. Within their own preparation meetings, the founding group members—who had received a planning grant—expressed concern that their role as lead or initiating partners could create an impression that they had resources to distribute that were simply not available. In response, the community members, volunteers, parents, and nonprofit members appeared to understand and express awareness of the limited budget and the need to obtain additional financial resources. It is also important to note that all of the partners were slightly uncomfortable with the financial aspects of the process. They wanted to know if they would be required to contribute money.

Gradually, small resentments grew over the seeming incongruence between the mantra "we have no money" and the perceived resources. The community college, university, and government planning group members noted that they had encountered several brutal years of budget cuts and that their cash flow, particularly unrestricted funding, was at an all-time low. Even though they were able to secure a $100,000 planning grant, the founding groups members felt they were in a resource-scarce environment. In conversation at the planning meetings, the leaders were vague about the amount of money they had, leaning perpetually on the phrase "we have no money." These founding members felt they were acting with integrity by being open about their financial situation and the resources they could offer. They did not consider the planning grant to be a significant source of revenue.

Community partners—notably the nonprofit groups—had a different perspective. Many were volunteers who were not attached to a specific organization, so their only tangible resources were time and information. Even inexpensive, in-kind items such as photocopying were absorbed as personal expenses. When community members attended planning meetings, they observed others as having office space, equipment, support staff, access to technology, and promotional items such as T-shirts and coffee mugs representing their respective institutions. The planning grant also paid for group meals and incidental expenses, perpetuating the notion that resources were available. The fact that the initial planning grant flowed through the university added to the perception that the postsecondary and government partners had money and resources.

As tensions built, there appeared to be an impasse. The community college, university, and government partners felt that the community members perceived them as money-bags, having resources that simply were not there. They also felt there was a subtle thread of envy or resentment about their supposed privileged status. Conversely, the community members believed that university and government members were insensitive and unaware of what it really meant to "have no money." This tension added to a growing sense of distrust or uneasiness. Fraser (1997) discusses similar tensions that develop when community members partner with school or government agencies. He notes that the perception of a class divide leads to a cycle of perceived neediness or disadvantage that disrupts the overall group cohesiveness and sense of collective power.

How did the partnership resolve these issues? One of the community partners questioned the university and community college partners' repeated statements about their financial situation. With support from the community members, this individual explained that when community members said *they* had no money, it literally meant there was no money. The member went on to say that the community was confused and upset by what appeared to be a dishonest representation of the situation by the community college and university partners, in part because of differing interpretations of the role and extent of the planning grant funds. This conversation led to more in-depth group analysis of what each person meant in using certain phrases or terms, and their contextual frame or lens. This single conversation moved the group to a much more positive frame. Perhaps most important, group members were willing to acknowledge that their words and actions could be variously interpreted by other members of the partnership. This acknowledgment caused them to slow down and explain their positions and concerns in greater detail and openness. As a result of more substantive and open conversation, the larger group focused on developing funding strategies for their planned project.

Discussion

The issues identified in this case study are ones that appear in the existing literature on community partnerships (Anderson and McFarlane, 1996; Baum, 2000). As Prins (2005) notes, tensions are inherent in the community-university partnership process. However, conflict can also offer opportunities for clarification and enhanced collaboration, so long as participants are able to work through the issues. In this case, the temporary communication snafus created a chance to improve collaboration. Though the early use of language such as *grassroots, mutual collaboration,* and *we have no money* did not appear to be loaded and was quickly accepted by all, the partners soon realized that their respective context shaped their understanding of these words. The rush to shared understanding can also be explained as an eagerness for an early bonding mechanism. Participants in new partnerships are looking for clues about what they have in common.

When tensions arose, those with competing perspectives overreacted and perceived disagreement as betrayal. The early bonding and belief that they were on the same page because of the similar language made the situation worse. Yet the group was able to slow down the communication process and in the end move forward on a largely successful project. Huxham and Vangen (2000) stress that group membership and organizational context shape interpretations; differences in language will add difficulty.

Recommendations

In beginning a new partnership or group project, it is important to recognize that even if group members use similar language they may in fact have differing understandings of the situation. When possible, set the tone by demonstrating willingness to clarify early discussions and ensure that all those present have an opportunity to participate. Recognize that an open communication system is a critical element of any partnership process, and it takes purposeful, consistent attention to make this happen (Bernal, Shellman, and Reid, 2004). Next, consider that organizational cultures may attach differential values to who participates and how. Regardless of organizational type, there is a natural tendency to look for reinforcement through equivalence or sameness. For example, if program directors are guiding a project for one partner, they look for a "director's equivalent" from other partners as a sign of respect and a basis for the assumption that it will be a smoother process if everyone is at the same level.

Collaborative advantages often happen in unexpected ways, and successful partnerships and shared risk can be negotiated in a number of novel and nontraditional manners. As part of the communication process, even if there are initial concerns it is possible to build in discussion of what potential participants bring to the table and how they will be included in the process.

References

Amey, M. J. and Brown, D. F. "Interdisciplinary Collaboration and Academic Work: A Case Study of a University-Community Partnership." In E. G. Creamer and L. R. Lattuca (eds.), *Advancing Faculty Learning Through Interdisciplinary Collaboration.* New Directions for Teaching and Learning, no. 102. San Francisco: Jossey-Bass, 2005.

Anderson, E. T., and McFarlane, J. M. "The Process of Community as Partner." In J. Brogan and V. Barishek (eds.), *Community as Partner: Theory and Practice in Nursing.* Philadelphia: Lippincott, 1996.

Baum, H. "Fantasies and Realities of University-Community Partnerships." *Journal of Planning Education and Research,* 2000, *20*(2), 234–246.

Bernal, H., Shellman, J., and Reid, K. "Essential Concepts in Developing Community-University Partnerships. CareLink: The Partners in Caring Model." *Public Health Nursing,* 2004, *21*(1), 32–40.

Fraser, N. "From Redistribution to Recognition? Dilemmas of Justice in a 'Postsocialist' Age." In N. Fraser (ed.), *Justice Interruptus.* New York: Routledge, 1997.

Huxham, C., and Vangen, S. "Ambiguity, Complexity and Dynamics in the Membership of Collaboration." *Human Relations,* 2000, *53*(6), 771–806.

Prins, E. "Framing a Conflict in a Community-University Partnership." *Journal of Planning Education and Research,* 2005, *25,* 57–74.

Tett, L. "Partnerships, Community Groups and Social Inclusion." *Studies in Continuing Education,* 2005, *27*(1), 1–15.

Tett, L., Crowther, J., and O'Hara, P. "Collaborative Partnerships in Community Education." *Journal of Education Policy,* 2003, *18*(1), 37–51.

SUSAN J. BRACKEN is an assistant professor of adult education at North Carolina State University.

NEW DIRECTIONS FOR COMMUNITY COLLEGES • DOI: 10.1002/cc

5

This chapter describes a partnership among a K–12 school district, a community college, and a four-year university. It focuses on the role that capital in various forms plays in the partnership.

Stepping Outside the Big Box High School: A Partnership Influenced by Goals, Capital, and Decision Making

Jesse S. Watson

This chapter examines a partnership that developed among a superintendent, a community college administrator, and a four-year college administrator to deliver secondary and postsecondary education to a Midwestern high school district and its neighboring communities. This partnership helped transform the process of transition from high school to postsecondary education from one that was segmented and hierarchical to one that is collaborative. Specifically, the partnership helped create a unique high school that rethinks what high school should look like. Within this case study, I highlight the work of three key individuals, paying particular attention to how they use various forms of capital to promote the partnership.

Throughout this chapter, I discuss several theoretical constructs to describe how the institutional actors achieve their goals. I pay particular attention to the concepts of capital and partnership. Capital has been described as a resource one uses to facilitate action (Coleman, 1988). There are a number of forms of capital, including social capital and organizational capital, which may not be evenly distributed among partners. *Social capital* refers to the use of social relationships or networks to obtain other resources of value (Coleman, 1988). The concept of partnership is related to that of relational capital and is based on the proximity of the exchanges between partners (Kale, Singh, and Perlmutter, 2000). For the purposes of

New Directions for Community Colleges, no. 139, Fall 2007 © 2007 Wiley Periodicals, Inc.
Published online in Wiley InterScience (www.interscience.wiley.com) • DOI: 10.1002/cc.292

49

this chapter, goals are individual or collective desired outcomes held by one or more of the related individuals.

In this chapter, I discuss several facets of this partnership among a high school, a community college, and a four-year university. I begin by discussing the context for the partnership and the partnership itself. I then describe how the institutional actors use various forms of capital to strengthen the partnership.

Situating the Partnership

Before discussing the partnership, it is critical to discuss the context in which it exists. Within this particular community, a decision was made to build a new high school. But local policy makers and legislators wanted to ensure that the newly built high school met the needs of the changing student population and the new economy. According to the superintendent of the K–12 school district, the high school was designed to ensure that the students of the county were able to graduate with a pertinent and contemporary set of skills: "We were trying to make sure that we didn't misfire and build a big-box, comprehensive high school that didn't have something new and different, given the world into which students are now graduating." The world to which the superintendent refers is one that requires a new approach to education, information, and development of informed individuals.

The county in which the high school resides also plays a significant contextual role in its development. According to the superintendent, "We are in transition as a community, but the history is that many of our students didn't have either the wherewithal or the predisposition to enroll in college full-time." The high school has also been designed to serve as a common facility for community use. As the superintendent explained: "We envision this school as being a kind of educational center for the community. I think that this will be a place that people visit for a variety of reasons." Those reasons range from fitness center membership to community programming to lifelong education through attendance of community and four-year college courses.

To fulfill this vision, the partnership worked to develop a new kind of high school, incorporating community college coursework and links to the four-year institution. The high school is still being developed, but it contains multiple physical wings that house various portions of the high school and the other postsecondary institutions. The high school will have a ninth grade academy that facilitates an easier transition into the high school environment. Tenth graders will be clustered into four courses according to academic interest. Additionally, the eleventh and twelfth graders will have the opportunity to take courses in a flex schedule format so that they can also take college courses simultaneously. The flex schedule allows better use of the high school facilities by offering postsecondary courses in the afternoon and evening, times when traditional high schools typically are dormant. The wings for the postsecondary institutions include office space for faculty and

NEW DIRECTIONS FOR COMMUNITY COLLEGES • DOI: 10.1002/cc

staff as well as classroom space related to the specifications of the individual institution. The high school will also include an open access library, a theater, and a concert hall; it is slated to have a fitness complex with a swimming pool.

The physical and conceptual space of the high school has become the backdrop for this partnership and subsequent interplays of individual and collective goals, capital, and sense making. Along with the unique theoretical and material arena I have described, there is also a requisite cadre of players that make exploration of the partnership possible.

The Partners

Although the web of relationships that guides and links these partners together is expansive, I focus on three key individuals: Brandon, the K–12 superintendent; Kyle, a community college administrator; and Ellen, a four-year university outreach administrator. They bring multiple and differing goals, capital, and perspectives that interact with one another against the backdrop of this new high school.

Brandon is a K–12 superintendent for the suburban school district (SSD); he seeks to better serve students through redefinition of the high school experience. In his work, he hopes to bring more opportunities for economic and personal prosperity to the youths of his school district. Kyle, the community college administrator, describes Brandon as "a really good leader. He has a lot of vision and likes to do things that are really in the best interests of the students and wants to do things differently. He really wanted to make this new high school different and better." Brandon firmly believes that inclusion of the college faculty and curriculum on the high school campus will have a tremendous effect on students: "When you put [postsecondary education] in the school, it becomes a very real presence for those students to see 'This is where I am going and this is what is before me, this is what is required of me.'"

Brandon is unique among the three players, given that he is the head of the school district. By virtue of his position, he directs resources (including financial and human capital) toward the project. He also relies on his accumulated social and organizational capital to attract other players (community colleges and four-year institutions) to his project and obtain support and resources from the school district's board of trustees and the larger community (Brumbach and Villadsen, 2002; Keener, Carrier, and Meaders, 2002). Finally, Brandon is able to use his social and organizational capital to interact with the board of trustees and community members in ways that can garner necessary support and resources.

Kyle is a community college administrator for Metropolitan Community College (MCC) at a satellite campus in the county where Brandon's district is located; he has a strong desire to serve students by creating opportunities for access to postsecondary education: "I really want to see our students succeed and have more choices because many students need to work." Kyle sees his job as making "education more accessible and hopefully seeing more students go on and get their bachelor's degree." Kyle brings to the partnership his passion to serve students and an understanding of students' needs. However, given his position as a midlevel administrator at a satellite campus, he has limited organizational capital. His efforts are often inhibited by the restricted support he receives from the community college administration. Although the community college is interested in the partnership because of the potential for increased enrollment, waning support or withdrawal of support can stop Kyle's involvement at any moment. He does not have the same base of power or control of resources that Brandon's position affords.

Nonetheless, Kyle is adept at making connections and uses his social capital to convince others that the project is worthwhile. Kyle's efforts are not related to expansion of the community college or an increase in funding; he simply wants to give students access to postsecondary education and new opportunities. Speaking about Kyle and his role in the partnership, Brandon suggests that Kyle "has been extraordinary in his enthusiasm for this partnership. I would give him the lion's share of the credit because it would have been easy for [MCC] to have said no." In this partnership, Kyle assumes the role of champion through his belief in the project and his determination and optimism to see the partnership through to fruition.

Ellen is an outreach administrator at a public four-year school, Outreach State University (OSU), who wants to deliver educational programs to students across the state while advancing the mission of her institution. On Ellen's personality and reputation, Brandon says that Ellen "is the key driver. She's got more energy coming out of her . . . and she has been the architect of many of [OSU's] satellite campuses." Though Ellen is a midlevel administrator, she has support from her institution, resources at her disposal, and programmatic flexibility.

The president of OSU has committed numerous assets to delivering outreach-based programs, including allocation of full-time faculty and staff for this particular partnership. As Ellen points out, the president "has in fact put in a growth model to get additional staff. It will be a two-year average of increases, and as your student credit hours go up, then you can get a new faculty line." The aggressive posture of OSU has been fostered through incentive and bonus pay for members of the outreach team. Along with being adept at delivering programs across the state, Ellen and OSU are simultaneously establishing partnerships with the other K–12 institutions in Brandon's county. Through these efforts, OSU is delivering needed programs while ensuring that OSU continues to grow and prosper with a businesslike tenacity. Within this partnership, Ellen brings a successful track record of delivering distance education at satellite campuses and the financial and institutional support necessary to effectively execute such an endeavor.

To implement the new high school concept, Brandon needs the participation of several types of postsecondary institution and community-based organization, such as hospitals and private businesses. These community-based partners help the new high school function as both a community center and a stepping stone for graduating students to move seamlessly into the workforce. With the goals of the new high school being community-centered and seamless workforce transitions, the relationships among Brandon, Kyle, and Ellen are particularly important because they represent their respective institutions. Their interactions within the partnership context are formal and informal depending on the setting in which they take place, whether a phone call between any two of them or a public ceremony celebrating the multiple partners.

Decisions, Positionality, and Observations

How individuals involved in a cross-institutional partnership use their capital and make decisions depends partly on their goals, which may differ on the basis of positionality, situational context, and proximity of their organizational self to the formation of the partnership (Brumbach and Villadsen, 2002; Keener, Carrier, and Meaders, 2002). In this case study, it is clear that the partners wanted to aid student transition from one form of education to another, and ultimately to the workforce. Institutions can form networks to focus on transition points from K–12 to postsecondary education, from K–12 to the workforce, and from community colleges to the workforce (Bragg, 2000). The benefits each person and institution receives by assisting in the transition vary from being a visionary architect to creating more access with educational opportunities to furthering an institution's prestige. As with collaboration and partnership, various meanings and implications exist for those involved (Watson, 2000). A partnership is a dynamic interaction and relationship that is influenced by motivating factors. Motivators such as Kyle's passion, Brandon's vision, and Ellen's institutional mission can influence how and when social and organizational capital is used.

In this partnership, Brandon has many advantages in being the superintendent of SSD. He has much of the organizational capital needed to promote his vision for the high school in terms of local funding, land, and voter support. He is also cultivating relevant social networks (capital) with Kyle and Ellen and other community-based partners to fulfill his ultimate goals. Because of his position, he also can use his social and organizational capital to move the partnership forward. This is best evinced by Brandon describing initial meetings with various prospective institutional partners: "It was never really clear what would happen educationally between the colleges and universities and the public schools. . . . The whole theory of the school-business partnership was to not only advance an opportunity for the vendor or the business of record, in this case [MCC], but also to have some advantage and benefit to our students. That was a central component." In these early meetings, Brandon is in the advantageous position of gatekeeper because he has the social and organizational capital to grant entrance into the new high school, which is something of value to Kyle and Ellen's respective institutions.

Unlike Brandon, who is in a senior leadership position, Kyle is situated somewhere in the middle of his organization. His position may be viewed as hindering his ability to directly control the flow of financial and human capital. However, Kyle uses his position and resources to initiate the necessary momentum to maintain and strengthen this burgeoning alliance. Kyle created momentum by establishing a committee of community college department chairs to develop a vision of MCC's role in the partnership. Kyle also stated that he needed "to get all of our people on board, and we have started monthly meetings with department chairs and people who I think can move this vision forward, to talk about what that would look like."

Kyle's limited control of organizational resources is offset by his social capital. This is a clear demonstration of his use of personal relationships to facilitate action (Coleman, 1988). Kyle has been able to forge institutional and interinstitutional relationships by using professional and personal connections along with introductions on the basis of those preestablished relationships. When asked about being a key player in this partnership, Kyle responded: "Let me be clear. I see my role as creating a vision. I have very little official authority to make that vision happen, so that is why I have to work hard, very collaboratively because I have zero authority to say to anybody, 'Here is what this is going to look like.' So it is all about getting the people who need to buy into this to buy into it."

Kyle's use of social capital focuses on strengthening this partnership to foster better opportunities for students in the county: "I wanted to change the focus of what we do out here . . . so that students really had a path laid out." Kyle also views the interaction between MCC and the student as a partnership and wants to provide clearly articulated pathways so that students can see where they are heading academically and professionally. In creating clearly defined relationships, interinstitutionally and with students, Kyle seeks to strengthen MCC's transfer mission within the county: "My whole thing was, 'Let's build these partnerships so that they are very clear to the student' and that the student will have a seamless process to ensure a good experience." Kyle's positionality may be a weak link in the partnership chain because of the lack of direct control over requisite organizational resources, but in being cognizant of his position Kyle is able to compensate by developing and cultivating strong social and interpersonal networks.

Juxtaposed to Kyle is Ellen, who is positioned within her organization to make use of multiple forms of institutional assets in order to carry out her university's mission. Ellen is in an interesting position as the director of outreach programming at OSU. The university president has embraced an entrepreneurial doctrine, focused on delivering programs to any and all locations within the state. By entering into this partnership, Ellen and OSU are poised to gain access into a new area of the state in which they had little previous involvement and to a population that will soon be acculturated and encouraged to engage in postsecondary endeavors. With the support of OSU and its businesslike, entrepreneurial mentality, which serves as a form of organizational capital, Ellen sees the partnership as an opportunity to assist students who may not otherwise enter higher education while generating revenue for her office and institution. Ellen believes that this "is a niche that we can fill." In the long run, she thinks "that we will win here . . . and when I say win, we won't be the only win, but I do think we fill a particular niche. [OSU] is generally well regarded statewide." Ellen's decision making and the motivation to use available forms of social and organizational capital are influenced by her commitment to give students desirable educational programs and the need to further her institution's outreach in the state and its subsequent economic well-being.

Examining the web of relationships that connect these individuals and their respective institutions shows that they are, whether purposefully or inadvertently, educational brokers (Sink and Jackson, 2002). In this role, they serve as a conduit for educational opportunities in much the same way as community colleges have assisted myriad individuals with their progression into and through the educational system. Though the brokers may have their own underlying motives for using various forms of social and organizational capital, it is clear that they all acknowledge students and their success as an important motivator for entering the partnership along with sharing resources (Brumbach and Villadsen, 2002; Keener, Carrier, and Meaders, 2002) and facilities (McCord, 2002).

Concluding Thoughts

This case study depicts how a physical space such as a new high school can serve as a nexus for partnership development and growth. As such, the high school is an environment in which social and organizational capital is cashed in to promote growth of the partnership. We have seen how Brandon and Ellen are able to wield organizational capital to initiate and contribute to the growing partnership. We have also seen how Brandon and Kyle use personal and professional relationships to facilitate development of this network.

The high school imparts benefits to each partner, such as shared facilities, student access to postsecondary education, and long-term county prosperity. The prospect of shared facilities is an enticing benefit of partnership for academic institutions (McCord, 2002). As the benefit of shared facilities or resources is distributed among all participants, other reasons for being in partnership may vary (Watson, 2000) and be influenced by the goals and sense-making strategies members use (Weick, 1995). Reasons and goals range from creating avenues of broader student access to reinventing the concept of high school to furthering the reach of an institution and its economic well-being. In the end, for these prospective college-age students not having to leave the county may be an incentive that encourages college attendance; this may go far in guaranteeing all the participating institutions a steady stream of students for years to come.

References

Bragg, D. D. "Maximizing the Benefits of Tech-Prep Initiatives for High School Students." In J. C. Palmer (ed.), *How Community Colleges Can Create Productive Collaborations with Local Schools.* New Directions for Community Colleges, no. 111. San Francisco: Jossey-Bass, 2000.

Brumbach, M. A., and Villadsen, A. W. "At the Edge of Chaos: The Essentials of Resource Development for the Community College." *Community College Journal of Research and Practice,* 2002, 26(1), 77–86.

Coleman, J. S. "Social Capital in the Creation of Human Capital." *American Journal of Sociology,* 1988, 94, S95–S120.

Kale, P., Singh, H., and Perlmutter, H. "Learning and Protection of Proprietary Assets in Strategic Alliances: Building Relational Capital." *Strategic Management Journal,* 2000, 21, 217–237.

Keener, B. J., Carrier, S. M., and Meaders, S. J. "Resource Development in Community Colleges: A National Overview." *Community College Journal of Research and Practice,* 2002, 26(1), 7–23.

McCord, R. S. "Breaking the School District Boundaries: Collaboration and Cooperation for Success." *Education,* 2002, 123, 386–389.

Sink, D. W., Jr., and Jackson, K. L. "Successful Community College Campus Based Partnerships." *Community College Journal of Research and Practice,* 2002, 26(1), 35–46.

Watson, L. W. "Working with Schools to Ease Student Transition to the Community College." In J. C. Palmer (ed.), *How Community Colleges Can Create Productive Collaborations with Local Schools.* New Directions for Community Colleges, no. 111. San Francisco: Jossey-Bass, 2000.

Weick, K. E. *Sensemaking in Organizations.* Thousand Oaks, Calif.: Sage, 1995.

JESSE S. WATSON is a graduate research assistant in the Higher, Adult and Life-long Education Doctoral Program in the College of Education at Michigan State University.

PART TWO

Less-Than-Successful Experiences

6

This chapter discusses the experiences of five two-year colleges that formed a statewide alliance. It details how the motivation for joining the alliance varied among the college leaders and describes the challenges the partners faced.

Alliances Among Community Colleges: Odd Bedfellows or Lasting Partners?

Pamela L. Eddy

This chapter describes the experiences of five technology colleges and their attempt to partner. Institutions partner for a variety of reasons (Russell and Flynn, 2000), but resource sharing often serves as a key motivating factor (Brumbach and Villadsen, 2002; Keener, Carrier, and Meaders, 2002). Such was the impetus for development of the Connected Campuses of Technology (CCT), a partnership among five colleges of technology. The partnership for the colleges grew out of the need to secure resources and lobby against potential closure. Ultimately, the CCT identified areas of individual campus expertise that helped market the programs across the state and constitute the basis for online course sharing among the colleges.

The Context of the Partnership

A board of trustees governs and coordinates all higher education institutions within the state where the community colleges in this study are located, and a chancellor leads the central office organization that oversees the comprehensive system of colleges and universities. At the time of the CCT formation, a new political party took over state governance and was forced to make significant cuts to the state budget, some of which affected higher education. At the same time, the newly appointed trustees knew little of the role and function of the five colleges of technology. The combination of budget cuts,

NEW DIRECTIONS FOR COMMUNITY COLLEGES, no. 139, Fall 2007 © 2007 Wiley Periodicals, Inc.
Published online in Wiley InterScience (www.interscience.wiley.com) • DOI: 10.1002/cc.293

changes in the state leadership, and decline in enrollment at the five colleges of technology instigated a shift within the centralized system of higher education, and the colleges seemed a good target since they had small bottom-line contributions. By 1994, the situation was dire. Press releases around the state discussed the possibility of campus closures, causing a high level of distress on the individual campuses.

Prior to formation of the CCT, the five college presidents met informally to share information and discuss the external issues facing all of their institutions. This informal structure set in motion a joint effort to lobby state legislators and the central office to forestall the threat of imminent closures. Given the success of this group, the chancellor's office strongly encouraged the five colleges to develop a voluntary alliance. In 1996, the CCT was officially recognized as a consortium of the state's five colleges of technology. At its core, the CCT works to promote cooperation and specialization among the five colleges while reducing competition and duplication. As a consortium, the CCT focuses on enrollment, academic initiatives that emphasize creation of baccalaureate degrees, technology infrastructure, administrative efficiencies, and resource development.

Along with the charge for cooperation came funding incentives from the state. Initial funding was targeted at $3 million for the group per year for five years. The majority of these funds were allocated to development of distance learning infrastructure on all five campuses; the remaining funds were allocated to operations. However, it was not clear how the operation funds should be divided among the five institutions; this set the stage for conflict as the campuses debated the question. In describing the allocation of funding, one vice president of administration quipped, "It was like throwing a hunk of meat to a group of lions."

The CCT formalized its relationship through memoranda of understanding (MOU) developed for each college by members of the campus and the central office administration. The MOU established baseline data for each campus along with enrollment targets, areas of specialization, and annual progress reports required by the central office to share among the member colleges.

This chapter describes in detail the challenges the partners faced in developing the CCT. The data come from interviews conducted in 1999. I interviewed all five college presidents as well as a member of the leadership team on each campus and the CCT executive assistant. After discussing the challenges the CCT faced, I offer some recommendations for those interested in developing partnerships.

The Players

All the campuses are located in rural areas of the state, because the colleges of technology were founded with the purpose of extending technical and agricultural support throughout the state. Pseudonyms are used throughout this

NEW DIRECTIONS FOR COMMUNITY COLLEGES • DOI: 10.1002/cc

chapter to protect the identity of the leaders and campuses. The five partnering colleges can be viewed in two camps: the haves and the have-nots. Given the funding formula within the state that linked budget allocation to enrollment, the two largest campuses within the CCT had more financial resources than the others with their smaller enrollments and more severe budgetary problems. We shall call the colleges that had more resources Algonquin College and Mountain College; the campuses facing more challenges were Downstate College, Cabin State College, and Northern College of Technology.

Algonquin College. Algonquin has the largest enrollment of the five partner institutions and a large institutional budget based on the state's funding formula. Nonetheless, college enrollment declined steadily between 1990 and 1996. Accordingly, the president wanted to use the CCT to help increase enrollment while reducing costs. At the same time, the president felt that technical education was not receiving proper funding and wanted to use the CCT to lobby the legislature. As he noted, "The presidents got together and decided to align themselves to speak with more clout as five colleges." There would be power in numbers.

Although the Algonquin president was supportive of the CCT, he found the process of collaboration difficult. In our interview, he commented that "we are not near achieving goals. The bureaucracy to get new academic programs approved is a barrier." For example, the CCT effort to create joint programs was hindered by the centralized state approval process and the self-interest of the partner campuses. The president stated: "When the five college presidents ran their group, they could not get consensus. No one person would or could take the lead since each had to have the interest of their own campuses before the CCT." To help address this situation, the CCT hired an executive director in 1997 to act as a decision maker and serve as the final arbiter for resource and academic decisions.

At Algonquin, skepticism regarding the alliance ran high. As the president reflected: "Once the people saw the [CCT] was here to stay, they worked hard to come up with ideas. But when they found out that their ideas were not going to be used, they became disillusioned and avoided working on alliance issues." A vice president at Algonquin noted that lack of a formal structure within the CCT also contributed to the demise of the partnership. Despite their common goals, the vice president observed, the five campuses were acting independently. By 1999, the two largest, Algonquin and Mountain, wanted to leave the partnership. However, the provost of the state's central higher education office held a partnership planning meeting and said: "You guys are going to have the CCT whether you like it or not. If you don't like it, you should do something else and we'll find someone who does." Thus the original voluntary nature of the CCT was now mandatory.

Mountain College. Though his colleague at Algonquin suggested that the need to increase enrollment and cut costs spurred creation of the partnership, the president at Mountain College suggested that "fear drove the campuses to collaborate." Put another way, the individual campuses feared closure and fought for survival by forming an alliance to support one another. However, the president also noted divisions within the consortium developing soon after implementation. One group saw the alliance as a confederation focused on group benefits, and the other group felt that formation of the CCT was merely a step in a larger plan to dissolve the individual campuses and form one larger single institution with a "super" leader. The factions aligned on have and have-not campus identity. The smaller campuses were fearful of being subsumed and overshadowed by the larger colleges.

The president at Mountain College and his administrators were interested in controlling their own destiny; there was less interest in the overarching goals of the CCT. In general, individual faculty were not overly aware of the larger partnership among the colleges. They were involved in determining how to allocate funding, but not in working toward shared programming among the campuses.

When discussing major barriers to success, the president noted that there was a disconnect between the consortium and the faculty and staff at the individual institutions. He suggested that "the process was driven centrally versus locally." Individual campus members were disconnected from the rationale for the collaborative beyond the single issue of preventing closure. The president of Mountain College indicated that the college's strategic plan did not include items specific to the CCT. The president also noted that it was challenging to deal with faculty and staff who were unconvinced or resistant to the consortium. The president said he worked to promote the consortium among his campus constituency, but ironically the examples he offered highlighted efforts under way on his own campus and not in conjunction with the CCT, underscoring the lack of buy-in to the CCT. For instance, instead of describing the course sharing taking place with the other four campuses he talked of new programs in his college's equine department for computer tracking of race horses, and new entrepreneurial programs under way in the agricultural programs focused on a storefront business.

Downstate College. In 1999, the president of Downstate College was new to the campus, having arrived on campus only in August of that year. The campus had witnessed a 20 percent decline in enrollment between 1990 and 1996, and the college was definitely in the have-not category of colleges under review. The president's perceptions were those of an outsider to the process, given her short tenure on the campus. Her initial view of the partnership was one of frustration; Algonquin and Mountain College wanted to leave the consortium. "Now they don't want to play anymore, they are taking their toys and leaving," she noted, referring to the amount of funding for the distance learning infrastructure received in the three previous years.

As a new leader in the CCT, she was unclear about its function and purpose. Her biggest question centered on the unclear mission for the group. She mentioned that formation of the group "allowed for more clout and a bigger stick" in dealing with the central office. Beyond this, she noted that the funding helped subsidize campus upgrades but offered little other commentary regarding the mission focus of the CCT.

The vice president of administration was present at the time of the CCT formation and described the first year as one of "semicontrolled chaos." This person recounted that the personalities of the presidents were an intervening factor, reflecting on how the strong leaders at Algonquin and Mountain College wanted to back out of the partnership. Even though the executive director at the central office "directed the colleges to work it out," the vice president indicated that "people were still holding their cards close to their chest."

Picking up on the relationship tensions, the vice president of academics at Downstate College added, "The CCT was not always a happy marriage." The central office's directive to "play nice" resulted in little change in relationships. For Downstate to succeed, it needed to align itself to the CCT's success. According to the academic vice president, the "message was not always clear, and what was needed was leadership." What was evidenced was strong individual campus leadership rather than a leader representing the interests of all five colleges and the CCT. The vice president noted that although the "CCT is a bright spot since there was power in numbers and there were benefits to working together," the money alone was not enough to keep the group focused on the goals of the CCT.

Cabin State College. In our interview, the president of Cabin State College offered that "the fear at the time of the formation of the CCT was that all five colleges would be consolidated into one single college." Given this fear, many on Cabin State's campus were skeptical of the partnership. Even though the college benefited from the relationship, many felt the partnership was castelike, with Cabin State being in the lower caste because of its smaller enrollment.

The president reflected that one key to survival was evolution. The CCT allowed the campus leaders to build on the strengths of the colleges. Autonomy of the individual campus was important in the initial stages of the CCT, but there was tension when the colleges "recognized the need to cooperate." A difficulty was that the colleges had no experience with a cooperative arrangement and did not know how to change the practice of being competitors.

Interestingly enough, the president of the faculty union at Cabin State College painted a slightly different picture of the CCT process. She argued that "the president acted like the CCT was forced on them, and then we find out that the colleges do not understand what to do about the collaboration." Moreover, the faculty felt there was undue secrecy around the CCT formation process. Many assumed that having a single president for all five campuses was an end goal. The college president perpetuated this assumption, which in turn shaped the faculty members' perception of the situation. As it turned out, there were really no plans for campus merger.

There was frustration regarding implementation of the CCT, but also the potential for real collaboration. For example, the faculty governance council supported the CCT goals of an increase in academic standards and development of baccalaureate of technology degree. A concern, however, was the loss of individual campus identity once portions of the degree were shared between campuses. A faculty member said, "There was no honest dialogue." Despite the influx of funding for distance learning initiatives, "no one checked whether the courses were needed or not." Lack of a coordinated effort to appropriately sequence class offerings left a jumble of assorted classes that did not result in any specific degree attainment.

Finally, the faculty at Cabin State did not see other campus faculty or programs as competitors, as campus leaders may have, but they did label Mountain College as the "rogue campus." This moniker appeared when the CCT was working on promoting laptop programs for all participating colleges and the president of Mountain College jumped the gun, implementing a campus laptop initiative unilaterally. The Cabin State faculty union president also noted that long-time faculty members were reluctant to change and embrace the CCT. In general, faculty felt their voices were not heard, resulting in a schism between administration and faculty regarding the CCT.

Northern College. The president of Northern College told the tale of the inception of the CCT, indicating the rocky moments already noted. He pointed out that the consortium reached a goal of developing a common mission statement; in addition, the funding given to the CCT "was something we could never have done alone." Yet a key fear remaining on campus was loss of individual identity. The president attempted to address concerns of the faculty by way of faculty meetings and open dialogue. He viewed empowering faculty to have control over aspects of the change process as paramount.

Nevertheless, the process for program approval was tedious through the centralized state system. The bureaucracy involved approval by all colleges in the state and final approval by the central system. These steps slowed the process of quickly implementing new baccalaureate programs and developing any type of shared degree option. The president described the CCT process as "trying to turn a battleship in a bad storm: you go into a wave and are not sure you are going up or not. It is like a near-death experience." Ultimately, the president felt his main concern about a single campus structure would turn into a reality, resulting in loss of individual campus uniqueness: "From a distance, the CCT looks good, but in reality the process has been messy." Part of the difficulty involved the tension among the member campuses: "The campuses wanting to get out of the CCT [Algonquin and Mountain College] are still causing trouble."

Tension

From the preceding description of the CCT, it is clear that there were a number of tensions within the partnership. Initial enthusiasm for the partnership was tempered by the reality of having to relinquish elements of control and lack of a clear champion for the process (Wolverton, 1998).

Individual campus leaders brought a sense of their own power to the relationship through their personality and background. Additionally, the campuses as units brought power differential to the CCT on account of their resource base, enrollment numbers, strength of academic programs, and location within the state (Fisher, 1984; Strauss, 1978). The leaders of Algonquin and Mountain College had more perceived power in the consortium given their resource base, ability to cope with uncertainty, and interpersonal campus alliances and networks (Morgan, 1998). Because these two campuses had more resources than the others, they had less incentive to participate in the CCT. Whereas the partnership was based on the espoused value of equality, it was clear this did not exist in practice. As one leader noted, "Yeah we're equal, but we knew we were better." A vice president at Algonquin went so far as to say that the three resource-scarce institutions were dragging down the college. Clearly, members at Algonquin felt they were bearing the burden of lifting up other campuses and not receiving enough benefits from the collaboration.

The shift from a voluntary partnership to a required one also changed the dynamic of the group. When individual presidents felt that they were banding together to prevent closure, there was a sense of shared duty and goals. Once the partnership felt required, questions were raised regarding the value of the collaboration to their campus. In particular, tensions rose after the imminent threat of closure was gone and the colleges had spent the influx of funding allocated to create the CCT. Despite the hiring of an executive director for the CCT, this person did not have the power to rein in the separate interests of the colleges, as evidenced by the inability to get full cooperation of all campuses to fulfill the goals of the CCT.

Another demarcation of the demise of the CCT was Mountain College's decision to go it alone with a laptop program. As previously mentioned, Mountain implemented a laptop initiative that was being discussed within the partnership and planned systemwide. The fact that the president unilaterally decided to implement this project showed a lack of buy-in to the consortium efforts. Moreover, there were no real repercussions to Mountain College for this act, which reinforced the notion that the partnership and executive director were ineffective in monitoring group activity. The singular action undermined any feelings of collaboration. Kotter and Cohen (2002) discussed how successful change initiatives require shared vision and buy-in to obtain lasting change. Clearly, these features were missing in the CCT. The campuses may have shared the vision of increasing efficiency and working toward the baccalaureate degree option, but they did not have shared understanding of what this meant or a shared level of buy-in to the process of attaining the outlined vision goals.

Finally, lack of an early official leader in the CCT meant that there was no clear champion of the process (Wolverton, 1998). It was not until 1999 that an executive director was named at the central office. Until that time, individual presidents rotated as the designated leader of the CCT. Although the structure of sharing responsibility for leadership in a partnership may be a means to gain buy-in, this was not the case for the CCT. Thus if a person felt less support for the CCT, he or she was less inclined to perform activities to support this work. By the time a centralized leader was named in the central office, the damage was done.

Outcomes

When one looks at the outcomes, clear successes are evident. Most noteworthy is the fact that all five campuses are still open. Even though the interim executive director commented that "there was no real threat of closure given the political climate," the colleges felt the threat was not an idle one. Changes in the state political system created a climate in which campus leaders were not sure whether the colleges would remain open. If a situation like potential closure is raised, the participating colleges may yet interpret and make sense of the situation according to their past experiences with the CCT (Weick, 1995).

Another clear benefit of the partnership was the influx of funding that allowed the five campuses to update their distance learning technology and begin to share classes, not only among the five campuses but through the statewide online course sharing program. The increase in shared information across the campuses enabled individuals at many levels to develop their own partnerships. Sadly, the majority of these lower-level collaborations were not sustainable once individual campuses tried to disband the CCT or make unilateral decisions that dampened motivation. The loss of funding prevented the intercollege teams from meeting because they did not have supporting resources.

Identification of specialty areas for individual campuses was helpful in marketing the colleges. However, this specialization proves challenging if one campus has a desire to begin or expand a program for which another campus is designated as the host institution, given their assigned area of expertise. Efficiency dictates that the campus deemed best at offering the program should continue to get the resources to support it. The distant locations of the five colleges and the de facto status of each as its region's community college meant students would not really have access to a full range of programming because the campuses were not within commuting distance and the full program was not available online.

A recent Web search for the CCT within the state's centralized system and on the individual campus Websites did not result in any hits. It appears that the formal partnership is now dissolved even though it operated from inception in 1996 to at least the signing of the MOUs in 2000, including the time period when interviews were conducted in 1999. The failure to sustain the partnership may mean several things. First, the partnership dissolved because its initial goals were met—namely, the CCT prevented the closure of any of the five colleges of technology. Second, the group collaborative did not share common goals or mission beyond the prime concern of staying open. Lack of a shared mission resulted in individual campuses believing institutional goals should supersede those of the collaborative. Finally, the absence of a clear champion for the alliance prevented the partnership from obtaining traction.

Lessons Learned

In considering the outcomes of the CCT partnership, one might argue that it was a success. The colleges remained open, which was not a guarantee in the mid-1990s. All the campuses received an infusion of funding to shore up their infrastructure, particularly for distance learning, and they developed new areas of unique programming. On the other hand, the potential for synergistic collaboration was lost thanks to the strong pull of protectionism among the individual campuses and unequal distribution of resources. Motivation and trust are critical to successful partnership, and the motivation for some campus leaders to participate in the alliance was less than for others.

The lessons learned by the five colleges can serve others contemplating a partnership. First, it is important to have clear objectives for the partnership. Even though the CCT was charged with a set of initial priorities that they cocreated with representatives from the state central office, these were defined differently according to the campus. For instance, enrollment development has one meaning when you are the largest campus in the partnership but another for the smallest. Thus not only clear objectives but also a shared understanding of what these objectives mean for each of the partners are required. It is critical to have shared goals for the partners. If we consider the shared goal of keeping the doors open on each campus, the partnership was a success. If we consider the larger goal of creating a statewide system of colleges of technology that appeal to niche markets and freely share among themselves, the partnership was a failure.

Second, feedback loops were missing for the consortium. With unrest evident early on, especially on the part of those at Algonquin and Mountain, it is important to have a group process for making adjustments within the partnership structure. A key component in establishing feedback loops is recognizing the critical element of relationship building. It is hard for a president to sell the concept of a partnership at his or her institution if the home campus constituents do not see the value of working together and instead view the partnership as a drain on their own resources.

Early motivation for cross-campus teams to establish benchmarks of best practice fostered a high level of communication. To sustain this exchange, it is important for participants to see that their efforts have a payoff. Kotter and Cohen (2002) refer to this as showing short-term wins. The shift from competitor to collaborator is hard to make in some instances, and the risk at early stages in a partnership is trusting other members to not use your cooperation against you. Yet fear is only a short-term motivator. Once any initial risk has passed, there needs to be longer-lasting reasons to participate.

Other community college leaders looking to establish partnerships can learn from the experience of the five colleges that participated in the CCT. Many partnerships are formed by happenstance, yet intentional planning of goals and objectives can serve all partners. Having a champion to help shape meaning and understanding for group members is critical to long-term success (Eddy, 2003; Fairhurst and Sarr, 1996). The manner in which presidential leaders use their power is also central to sustaining partnership (Fisher, 1984; Morgan, 1998). For those involved in a partnership or contemplating forming some type of collaboration, it is important to think holistically and systematically about the elements that add to the potential for success. Clearly, the role of the partnership leaders is critical for long-term success. Community college leaders can help by making sure that there is shared meaning of the goals and mission of the partnership and by providing feedback loops that permit adjustment as relationships change over time. These leaders can leverage the power of their position in planning and implementing academic partnerships.

References

Brumbach, M. A., and Villadsen, A. W. "At the Edge of Chaos: The Essentials of Resource Development for the Community College." *Community College Journal of Research and Practice,* 2002, 26(1), 77–86.

Eddy, P. L. "Sensemaking on Campus: How Community College Presidents Frame Change." *Community College Journal of Research and Practice,* 2003, 27(6), 453–471.

Fairhurst, G. T., and Sarr, R. A. *The Art of Framing: Managing the Language of Leadership.* San Francisco: Jossey-Bass, 1996.

Fisher, J. L. *Power of the Presidency.* New York: Macmillan, 1984.

Keener, B. J., Carrier, S. M., and Meaders, S. J. "Resource Development in Community Colleges: A National Overview." *Community College Journal of Research and Practice,* 2002, 26(1), 7–23.

Kotter, J. P., and Cohen, D. S. *The Heart of Change: Real Life Stories of How People Change Their Organizations.* Cambridge, Mass.: Harvard Business School Press, 2002.

Morgan, G. *Images of Organization* (2nd ed.). Thousand Oaks, Calif.: Sage, 1998.

Russell, J. F., and Flynn, R. B. "Commonalities Across Effective Collaboratives." *Peabody Journal of Education,* 2000, 75(3), 196–204.

Strauss, A. *Negotiations: Varieties, Contexts, Processes, and Social Order.* San Francisco: Jossey-Bass, 1978.

Weick, K. E. *Sensemaking in Organizations.* Thousand Oaks, Calif.: Sage, 1995.

Wolverton, M. "Champions, Agents, and Collaborators: Leadership Keys to Successful Systemic Change." *Journal of Higher Education Policy and Management,* 1998, 20(1), 19–30.

PAMELA L. EDDY *is associate professor in educational leadership at Central Michigan University.*

NEW DIRECTIONS FOR COMMUNITY COLLEGES • DOI: 10.1002/cc

7

This chapter presents lessons learned from a community college in Arizona in implementing dual-enrollment partnership programs.

Lessons Learned from a Dual-Enrollment Partnership

Patricia L. Farrell, Kim Allan Seifert

In this knowledge-based economy, state policy makers realize that a vital state resource is the intellect of its population (Campbell and Eckerman, 1964; Krueger, 2006). The U.S. Bureau of Labor Statistics estimates that a majority of the fastest-growing and highest-paying occupations require some form of postsecondary education. As a result, a high school diploma is no longer sufficient (Krueger, 2006). Policy makers are therefore looking at ways to develop human capital to improve economic development. In recent years, they have focused on P–16 education, by encouraging students to graduate from high school and attend college, increasing access to college, and making college more affordable (Carnevale and Fry, 2001).

Thus far, forty-seven state legislatures have developed dual-enrollment programs as a strategy to increase their states' human capital. These programs give high school students the opportunity to take postsecondary courses through two-year and four-year colleges and universities (Krueger, 2006). The programs are designed to promote rigorous academics; save students' time and money on a college degree; encourage competition among colleges and universities; increase student aspirations to go to college; and build closer ties among colleges, high schools, and their communities (Education Commission of the States, 2001). As it stands, state legislatures create the policies under which dual-enrollment programs operate. As a result, dual-enrollment programs vary considerably from state to state. Policies regarding tuition fees, eligibility requirements, faculty participation,

NEW DIRECTIONS FOR COMMUNITY COLLEGES, no. 139, Fall 2007 © 2007 Wiley Periodicals, Inc.
Published online in Wiley InterScience (www.interscience.wiley.com) • DOI: 10.1002/cc.294

enrollment, and academic rigor all vary by state (Karp, Bailey, Hughes, and Fermin, 2005).

Postsecondary institutions and high schools enter into dual-enrollment programs for well-intentioned reasons. However, the literature suggests that conflict sometimes develops from state policy or the relationship between partnering institutions. Dougan (2005) notes that some of the most common issues concern students' academic preparation, the availability of college student services, faculty preparation and training, and lack of formal evaluation measures. In this chapter, we address lessons learned by an Arizona community college that participated in a dual-enrollment program with several local high schools. The lessons learned include setting academic and faculty standards; coordinating the collaboration, understanding, and implementing of the policies; considering college preparation; and determining evaluation methods.

The Story

The community college studied is located in an urban region in Arizona; it has more than 350 full-time instructional and support staff. Seventy thousand students enroll annually at multiple campuses through degree and nondegree programs. Most of the college's students are enrolled part-time, and 40 percent are Hispanic or Native American. Forty-one percent of students are in a transfer program, 46 percent participated in an occupational or workforce program, and 8 percent take a developmental program.

In 1997, the school began offering courses for college credit in math and English to local high school students. College administrators thought the dual-enrollment program was running smoothly until they learned that local four-year postsecondary institutions refused to give credit to incoming students who took dual-enrollment classes at the community college. The four-year institutions were concerned that the dual-enrollment courses did not meet the rigor of college courses and did not prepare students for subsequent college courses. The fact that the instructors teaching the courses did not meet the community college standards for faculty employment was also problematic.

As a result, college administrators realized that they had to take a step back and evaluate the dual-enrollment program. First, they had to remind themselves that the program was designed to prepare students for higher education. Thus if students did not receive credit for the course at another postsecondary institution, dual enrollment was little more than a self-serving exercise for the college. College administrators also found out that high school principals and counselors were offering inaccurate information to parents about the dual-enrollment program; high school officials were telling the parents that the dual-enrollment and advanced placement programs were equivalent. Of course, parents learned that this was incorrect once their son or daughter enrolled in a postsecondary institution. According to Arizona state policy, high schools must inform students and families of dual-enrollment program opportunities. Unfortunately, in this case the parents were being given inaccurate information.

On the basis of these issues, the college administrators reorganized the dual-enrollment program, paying particular attention to enrollment issues, location of classes, and teaching standards. Administrators also made the decision to require high school students to take an assessment test in their junior year to qualify for the dual-enrollment courses. The assessment covers reading, writing, and math and seeks to demonstrate whether students are prepared for college-level courses. However, many high school administrators balked at the test requirement; they said they would find it embarrassing to inform parents that their children had not passed the college assessment test when the high schools were, ostensibly, grooming students with college preparatory classes. One private high school ended the relationship and found another postsecondary institution to teach dual-enrollment courses. That school has recently petitioned the community college to be allowed to resume its relationship under the new assessment requirements.

With the new model, administrators also require the students to take more responsibility for their academic future. Before taking the assessment test, students have to obtain permission to take the course from their parent or guardian, and from a high school counselor. After the test, they are required to meet with a college academic advisor. As a result of the higher standards and more rigorous college content classes, local four-year postsecondary institutions have begun to grant entering students credit for the dual-enrollment courses taken from the college.

Although the community college was able to address the concerns of parents, the high school, and four-year colleges and universities, it encountered resistance from an Arizona tax reform group that has been scrutinizing the state's funding for dual-enrollment programs. The group's concern is that schools (the community college and high school) are "double dipping." The tax group is partially correct in its assessment; Arizona policy states that both schools will be funded through the state government at their full FTE rate and that the student is not charged for tuition. The agreement this college has with the high schools is that it will pay for the tuition while the high school pays for the instructional costs. Similar funding patterns exist in other states as well. As a result of the tax advocacy group's pressure, the college administrators are lobbying the legislature each year to make sure they do not lose their full funding.

Lessons Learned

This story illustrates that before a community college and high school enter into a dual-enrollment partnership, administrators need to create a strategic plan that accounts for current legislation, best practices, and the needs of the community along with those of local high schools and postsecondary institutions. In this section, we discuss specific strategic areas related to academic standards, faculty standards, coordination, policy, and college preparation.

Academic Standards. As illustrated, this community college began offering dual-enrollment programs in 1997 without taking the time to create a solid plan that addressed the needs of students, high schools, and the community college. Consequently, college and high school administrators received a wake-up call when they learned that four-year institutions did not accept the dual-enrollment classes as transfer credit.

According to the Center for an Urban Future, approximately 30 percent of college freshmen need remedial classes. Consequently, it is critical for the three educational layers—high school, community college, and four-year university or college—to collaborate and agree on assessment tests, course curriculum, and preparation for subsequent courses of both the customary academic and dual-enrollment programs (Kleinman, 2001). The center calls for postsecondary institutions and high schools to work together to align standards and expectations. One dilemma is that K–12 policy makers test for what they think students should have learned, and postsecondary educators test for what they think students need to know before attempting college-level courses. Unless the institutions align these tests, "students and secondary schools will continue to receive a confusing array of signals, and will not be able to prepare adequately for higher education" (Kirst, 1999, p. 11). Kirst states that there is nothing inherently wrong with testing students. However, his point is that the education world is "blowing a golden opportunity to connect demanding tests—and curricula—in secondary schools with what colleges are looking for. Shared standards would allow schools to actually cut down on testing while at the same time improving student understanding of what is required of them if they want to succeed in college" (p. 11).

Dual enrollment can be a mechanism for aligning high school and postsecondary education, not merely a strategy for advancing students out of high school. The alignment of high school exit and test standards with college admission standards helps prepare all high school students for college-level learning. In this way, dual enrollment programs can be part of a larger P–16 agenda (Krueger, 2006). In addition to alignment of standards, partnerships between high schools and postsecondary institutions in rural or urban areas can also benefit because resources are usually scarce and funding is limited. They can profit by sharing resources and working collaboratively.

Faculty Standards. Four-year institutions raised the issue that the instructors teaching dual-enrollment courses in the high schools did not meet the criteria necessary to be a faculty member at the community college. However, it is important to note that community colleges hire more than half a million adjunct faculty to teach courses, some of which are dual-enrollment classes. Moreover, 67 percent of the faculty members at

NEW DIRECTIONS FOR COMMUNITY COLLEGES • DOI: 10.1002/cc

two-year institutions are adjuncts or part-time employees (Conley and Leslie, 2002). These part-time faculty members have a hidden value when teaching in technical and career areas in that they are often more current about the content in their fields, having stepped from their job directly into the classroom.

But to address the concerns of four-year institutions and better prepare the adjunct faculty, it is imperative for community colleges to develop teaching standards for all faculty. Opportunities for professional development in the areas of teaching and learning theory and practice need to be offered, in addition to implementing new ways of evaluating faculty's teaching methods in the classroom. This is an excellent opportunity for community colleges to partner with four-year institutions, which probably have a professional development unit or institute of teaching and learning for their faculty.

Coordination. This story illustrates how institutions often work independently. As noted in the Arizona story, the community college did not coordinate with four-year institutions to ensure the transfer of coursework; nor did it set up an articulation agreement. This lack of coordination created problems for both students and the community college. Therefore it is critical to create an ongoing collaborative environment, to confirm that the institutions are aligning standards at all levels and sharing those expectations with students, parents, and faculty. Coordination also creates opportunities to evaluate existing programs, so successful approaches can be replicated; and it ensures administrative resources are used effectively. According to Krueger (2006), it is the community college's responsibility to lead the coordination effort, ensuring easy transfer of course credit from high school to college, and then from community college to four-year institutions. This is an essential component of any successful dual-enrollment program.

Policy. Arizona's dual-enrollment law was implemented in 1984, allowing qualified high school students to take postsecondary education courses and community colleges to offer dual-enrollment courses at the high school. The state law declares that colleges can offer only certain courses for dual enrollment, teachers must have the same credentials as the college faculty, colleges must approve the course syllabus, and students do not have to pay for dual-enrollment classes because the school district and community college receive funding from the state for the student. However, state oversight is limited. In Arizona, the community college need only submit a list of courses and student outcomes each year. Thus, if the state had required and enforced what the law declares, several of the issues experienced among this community college, the high schools, and four-year institutions would not have occurred.

As dual-enrollment programs gain popularity, state policy makers need to carefully consider how to best design and evaluate these programs. Creating a mechanism for moving students through the system without paying attention to rigor or quality is a waste of student time and state resources. It is in the interest of both the student and the legislature to support and encourage implementation of dual-enrollment programs. For the student, transition to college is made more feasible if the program considers not only academic preparation but the social aspects of college. When dual-enrollment courses are offered on a community college campus and high school students are integrated with college students, they can become familiar with college life, both academically and socially. For the legislature, this is a more cost-effective means of delivering college-level classes.

As in the case of Arizona, the student does not have to pay for tuition and therefore can start preparing for college by gathering course credits without financial worries. Applying equitable financing mechanisms such as this helps ensure that low-income and underrepresented students are not excluded from dual-enrollment programs for inability to pay tuition (Krueger, 2006). States need to let students and parents, particularly low-income students, know what dual-enrollment options are available in their state through various information campaigns.

Finally, community college leaders need to be politically savvy and able to interpret complex laws. As noted, a tax group is trying to influence policy makers and the public to change dual-enrollment policies. The implication is that community colleges need to work with other educational institutions to understand issues and policies to ensure that they are operating properly under the laws and to lobby for the welfare of the students, community, and institutions.

College Preparation. High school academic achievement, social class background, and high school experience shape how students perceive their prospects for college. No student sees the opportunity of going to college in its entirety. Instead, students imagine schools that they judge "right" or "appropriate" or schools where they believe they will feel comfortable (McDonough, 1997). First-generation students, who typically are minority and low-income, usually have no one to help guide them through the labyrinth of searching and preparing for college. They are also less likely to understand the system in which they find themselves once they are enrolled. These are critical issues for postsecondary institutions to consider in increasing student access and retention (Harrell and Forney, 2003). Students who take dual-enrollment classes at a community college experience at least some version of college while in the protective cloak of high school. These students then have enough familiarity with the college system to no longer fear it and are capable of making a smoother transition into the college environment.

Once the student enters college, it is important to encourage and support academic and social assimilation as a means of promoting retention (Tinto, 1993). Research shows that freshmen students are especially susceptible to leaving college because of inadequate academic and social integration (Tinto, 1998). Thus offering dual-enrollment programs can assist students to prepare for college integration if classes are taught at the college campus and students have access to academic and student affairs opportunities.

NEW DIRECTIONS FOR COMMUNITY COLLEGES • DOI: 10.1002/cc

Little research on dual-enrollment programs addresses the importance of faculty in preparing future college students. The focus is primarily on credentialing and standards of faculty, and not on the effect they have on students. In her research on community college students, Rendón found that validation by faculty was critical in "transforming students into powerful learners," especially minority, low-income, first-generation, nonracial-minority, and female students (1994, p. 39). She recommends faculty learning how to recognize students as learners and connect with high school students. According to Rendón, faculty also need to be aware of the demographics of their students so they will understand the needs and strengths of a culturally diverse class of students and how to foster a validating classroom (Rendón, 1994).

Evaluation. Currently, states use three primary oversight processes for dual-enrollment programs: financial reporting, policy compliance, or quality control. Arizona's law for oversight involves quality control, requiring programs to report annually on course offerings and student outcomes. However, no long-term evaluation processes are required to learn about student access, retention, ability, and career aspirations. Given the importance of assessment, Arizona should follow students from high school through college, studying course-taking patterns and outcomes, student engagement, and the human capital impact within the state. In addition, evaluating the program will help colleges and schools improve their partnerships.

Conclusion

In this chapter, we addressed dual-enrollment programs and the inherent challenges that must be dealt with on the part of collaborating institutions. Practitioners should be aware of the challenges throughout the lifespan of the dual-enrollment agreement. A key factor leading to the success, or in its absence the failure, of a dual-enrollment program is an explicit understanding of the goals and motives of all parties involved. All constituents in the process—including the students—should examine and delineate their desired outcomes before becoming involved. With an open dialogue between participants, true collaboration can occur that will ultimately result in production of a stronger partnership.

Flexibility and understanding of each constituent's changing needs and the host institution's ability to provide services will positively affect the longevity and viability of the dual-enrollment program. As tertiary institutions' curriculum requirements change, the dual-enrollment program must be able to alter course offerings to meet those changes. Part of a community college's mission typically includes preparing students to transfer to a four-year institution, so accounting for the receiving institutions' requirements enhances the credibility of the dual-enrollment program.

Perhaps the most important characteristic of successful collaboration in a dual-enrollment program is a high level of communication among all parties. Recognizing that partners have differing agendas and goals, all participants must effectively communicate and actively seek to openly deal with exposed differences in vision and needs. Limitations in the ability of any partner to provide services should be discussed early in the process and alternatives found to maintain the integrity of the program. Overzealousness and overestimating the abilities of a partner to furnish required services can essentially doom the dual-enrollment program to failure.

Dual-enrollment programs offer high school students a means of advancing their educational career rapidly and in a direction of interest to them. Students intent on pursuing both a four-year degree and career technical education can benefit from a dual-enrollment program that is structured to meet their needs. The savings in time and often money for the student validates the continuing need and desirability of fostering and encouraging our community colleges' participation in these worthwhile programs.

In conclusion, if a state's goal is to increase human and social capital, then policy makers and P–16 administrators, faculty, and researchers need to come together to dialogue on how they can graduate better-prepared students. They need to collaborate on improving faculty training, strengthening curricula, and giving students the information and support they need to succeed.

References

Campbell, A., and Eckerman, W. C. *Public Concepts of the Values and Costs of Higher Education.* Ann Arbor: Survey Research Center, Institute for Social Research, University of Michigan, 1964.

Carnevale, A. P., and Fry, R. A. *Economics, Demography and the Future of Higher Education Policy.* Washington, D.C.: National Governors Association, 2001 (http://www.nga.org/cda/files/HIGHEREDDEMOECON.pdf; accessed May 1, 2007).

Conley, V. M., and Leslie, D. W. *Part-Time Instructional Faculty and Staff: Who They Are, What They Do, and What They Think.* NCES 2002–163. Washington, D.C.: U.S. Department of Education, 2002.

Dougan, C. P. "The Pitfalls of College Courses for High-School Students." *Chronicle of Higher Education,* 2005, *52*(10), B20.

Education Commission of the States. *Postsecondary Options: Dual and Concurrent Enrollment.* Denver, Colo.: Education Commission of the States, 2001 (http://www.ecs.org/clearinghouse/28/11/2811.pdf; accessed May 1, 2007).

Harrell, P., and Forney, W. "Ready or Not, Here We Come: Retaining Hispanic and First-Generation Students in Postsecondary Education." *Community College Journal of Research and Practice,* 2003, *27,* 147–156.

Karp, M. M., Bailey, T. R., Hughes, K. L., and Fermin, B. J. *Update to State Dual Enrollment Policies: Addressing Access and Quality.* Washington, D.C.: Office of Vocational and Adult Education, U.S. Department of Education, 2005 (http://www.ed.gov/about/offices/list/ovae/pi/cclo/cbtrans/statedualenrollment.pdf; accessed May 1, 2007).

Kirst, M. W. "A Babel of Standards: Students Face a Confusing Array of Tests and Assessments." *National Crosstalk,* 1999, *7*(4), 11–14.

Kleinman, N. S. *Building a Highway to Higher Education: How Collaborative Efforts Are Changing Education in America.* New York: Center for an Urban Future, 2001.

Krueger, C. *Dual Enrollment: Policy Issues Confronting State Policymakers.* Denver, Colo.: Education Commission of the States, 2006.

McDonough, P. M. *Choosing Colleges: How Social Class and Schools Structure Opportunity.* Albany: State University of New York Press, 1997.

Rendón, L. "Validating Culturally Diverse Students: Toward a New Model of Learning and Student Development." *Innovative Higher Education,* 1994, *19*(1), 33–51.

Tinto, V. *Leaving College: Rethinking the Causes and Cures of Student Attrition.* Chicago: University of Chicago Press, 1993.

Tinto, V. "Colleges as Communities: Taking Research on Student Persistence Seriously." *Review for Higher Education,* 1998, *21*(2), 167–177.

PATRICIA L. FARRELL *is the executive director of the Association for the Study of Higher Education, headquartered at Michigan State University.*

KIM ALLAN SEIFERT *is department chair for business and marketing at Doña Ana Community College, Las Cruces, New Mexico.*

NEW DIRECTIONS FOR COMMUNITY COLLEGES • DOI: 10.1002/cc

8

This chapter explores issues surrounding the demise of the Interdisciplinary Master's in Education (IMED) program, which was delivered on the neighbor islands in the state of Hawai'i. The innovative program brought educational opportunities to remote areas of the state and was a partnership between the main campus in Honolulu and several community colleges.

A Partnership in Flux: The Demise of a Program

Gay Garland Reed, Joanne E. Cooper, Llewellyn Young

Organizational theorists, especially those using a systems approach, assert that organizations have a life cycle that includes birth, growth, death, and an opportunity for renewal near the end of the cycle (Adizes, 1996, 2004; Bridges, 2003). This is the story of just such a birth and death. The entity was a complex partnership that involved faculty from seven College of Education departments and four community colleges around the state of Hawai'i.

We share this story with the hope that the death of this innovative and valuable program will be instructive to the reader. We begin with a description of the program and its collaboration with the community colleges on the neighbor islands of Hawai'i. Our frameworks are borrowed from Bridges (2003) and Morgan (1998), whose work illuminates aspects of our story. We then tell the tale impressionistically from the perspectives of three people who taught in the program. In this context, impressionist tales (Cooper, Brandon, and Lindberg, 1998; Van Maanen, 1998) offer first-person accounts from faculty who participated in the partnership and viewed their experiences from varying perspectives within the program. It is important to note that these tales are not necessarily representative. Nor do they permit scholarly analysis of the demise of the program. Rather, they are tales from the heart illuminating the personal and professional significance that can be gleaned from being part of a collaborative process. The reader may think of them as journalistic sketches from the perspectives of three people

whose journeys were intertwined and enhanced through participation in this program.

The primary theoretical frame comes from Bridges (2003), who suggests that organizations have a life cycle of seven stages. The first stage he calls *dreaming the dream,* which is the time of imagining and planning. The second is *launching the venture,* the time when the organization is in its infancy. From there, the next stages are *getting organized, making it,* and *becoming institutionalized.* These are the times of active engagement, moving toward adulthood, and becoming part of the institutional landscape. The last two phases, *closing in* and *dying,* are sometimes brought about by "an increasingly unresponsive bureaucracy" (p. 81). Bridges also posits the possibility of renewal and beginning anew if conditions allow rejuvenation by capturing the energy of the first three stages. Although the potential for renewal marked the closing-in stage of our program, it was not realized, for several reasons that are discussed later.

The Interdisciplinary Master's of Education Program

The Interdisciplinary Master's of Education (IMED) program was born out of a need to deliver graduate education to the isolated populations of students on neighbor islands in Hawai'i. This island state is one of the most remote places on earth in terms of distance from a major continent, and distance sometimes raises issues of access and equity for students.

When the IMED was created, professional development was possible only through a piecemeal approach that involved taking an occasional course at the local community college or spending a summer in Honolulu attending the university. Occasionally, more determined students would fly to Oahu once a week to attend evening classes, but the need to serve neighbor island populations continued to grow. Eventually, political pressure gave way to legislative allocations to establish programs for the underserved population on the island of Kauai. The IMED program was conceived to fill this need.

During the life cycle of the program, we served communities of various degrees of remoteness and came to understand the constraints facing those who lived on the periphery of the periphery. Although we took the program to neighbor islands and saw ourselves as reaching out to underserved parts of the state, we learned that many students lived in remote parts of the island or even came from nearby islands, traveling a long distance by car or ferry to attend class. This issue of differential educational access within a remote community brought inherent inequities into focus. Sometimes the extra burdens faced by students who came from a great distance were transformed into ways of strengthening community, as when the in-town people hosted the out-of-town people over a long weekend or people from the periphery drove in together and used that time as an opportunity to foster connectedness. Nevertheless, for the students who lived on the periphery of the periphery the program was particularly taxing, reminding the faculty that people make remarkable—often invisible—sacrifices to attain educational rewards. In distance education, the variety of models and the complexity of adapting to changing environments and conditions can be both invigorating and challenging. To some degree, the system ecology depends on finding ways to balance resources and nurture connectedness.

A Systemwide Partnership

The University of Hawai'i System includes ten campuses spread around the state on five main islands. The College of Education is part of the main campus at Manoa in Honolulu. Throughout the life of the IMED program, the college worked closely with community colleges and centers on four neighbor islands. This unique relationship presupposes a high level of cooperation between the Manoa programs and the neighbor island sites. It includes designated personnel on each island responsible for some degree of coordination with representatives from Manoa programs. Students have access to library databases through the university's Voyager system, which extends academic support for student research. Maui Community College and Kauai Community College both have libraries that offer interlibrary loan for students in their communities who need reference materials from the main library in Honolulu. Additionally, centers on the big island of Hawai'i and on Moloka'i have computers available for students who do not have access. Real-time transmission of classes from one island to another is possible through interactive television. This was particularly useful in the dual-island cohort when some classes were held in Kona and broadcast to Moloka'i and some classes were held on Moloka'i and broadcast to Kona. The logistical, academic, and distance technology links are all in place to make the process a smooth one.

Finally, the community colleges offered steady support and dedicated service throughout the IMED program. For example, during the last class on a Saturday the entire sound system in the interactive television studio broke, leaving the teaching faculty member with only visual contact with half her students. The director of technology at the community college came into the center to troubleshoot and make repairs, even though it was his day off. This is just one example of the hard work and dedicated support of the community colleges throughout the program.

The Life and Death of a Program

Located at the main campus in Honolulu, the University of Hawai'i College of Education was pressured by legislators to supply island-bound teachers with continuing and graduate education. In 1994, a legislator from Kauai convinced the state legislature to provide $172,000 for professional development in the form of graduate education on her island. This was Bridges's dreaming the dream stage (2003). It was followed closely by the second stage, launching the venture, which took place in the fall of 1995.

During the IMED launching phase, faculty from seven of the college's departments (Educational Foundations, Educational Psychology, Educational Administration, Counseling and Guidance, Curriculum and Instruction, Educational Technology, and Special Education) came together to develop the program and build the curriculum. The college decided to house the program in the Educational Foundations Department, which had a welcoming faculty with a track record for designing innovative programs. It was also an interdisciplinary program, so it seemed like a natural place to house the IMED. (The significance of being "housed" versus "having a home" is discussed later as one of the ecological factors that brought about the program's demise.)

In 1995, faculty met to design the curriculum, to be based partly on a needs assessment from potential students who lived on Kauai. At this point, there was great enthusiasm and energy for the project. Faculty, neighbor island teachers, and legislators were participating in the first three stages of organizational life as described in Bridges: dreaming the dream, launching the venture, and getting organized (2003).

The program was designed to focus on teacher leadership and served twenty students, most of whom were practicing teachers on Kauai. It took two years for students to earn a master's degree; they attended class on weekends during the school year and over an intensive period of time in the summer. Faculty traveled to Kauai, and in subsequent rounds to other neighbor islands, to deliver the courses at the community colleges on the several islands. The entire venture depended on cooperation with the community colleges of the state, which served as delivery sites and also as crucial players in the partnership. In total, the program delivered four rounds of master's curriculum: one to Kauai, two to Maui, and the final round jointly to the island of Moloka'i and the Kona area of the big island of Hawai'i, all areas that were underserved in terms of graduate education for teachers.

In the last round, faculty used interactive television studios located in the community colleges so that students on Moloka'i could be visually connected to their classmates in Kona and vice versa. The university faculty members alternated between locations; one week's course was delivered in Kona and the next week's in Moloka'i. The community colleges furnished some clerical support for the courses, as well as technicians to run the television studios. Advising and other necessary communication were conducted via email, before and after class, and in occasional individual-advisor meetings. Two of the students from Moloka'i had positions at the university center, so our partnership with the community college was enhanced.

In each round of the program, it was necessary to go through Bridges's third stage of getting organized. This involved recruiting students, deciding who would teach, and tailoring the curriculum to meet students' needs. During this time, some of the college's faculty rotated through the program, but the basic structure of the program remained the same. Faculty members were able to employ innovative curricular designs,

NEW DIRECTIONS FOR COMMUNITY COLLEGES • DOI: 10.1002/cc

such as a reflective course that spanned the entire two years of the program. This fourth stage of organizational life is called making it and is when the organization's adulthood begins. Soon IMED was into the fifth stage, becoming an institution where it was an accepted part of the college curriculum. In this phase, the program enjoyed success and prestige, thanks in part to the enthusiastic response from students and neighbor island administrators.

During the ten years in which these four rounds of master's degrees were awarded, the Department of Educational Foundations was also changing. The original chair had been teaching in the program and four other departmental faculty members were involved in the program during the initial stages. Gradually, some of these faculty members retired or left the program. This change in faculty contributed to the sixth stage, closing in. In this developmental stage, energy and attention turn inward and internal politics and changes in the organization command attention (Bridges, 2003). Bridges's description of the closing-in stage aptly relates what was occurring in the IMED near the end of its third round. During this period, a new department chair stepped in; this person was not invested in the program and felt that it competed with other iterations of the Educational Foundations master's program. Similarly, the dean felt the IMED program vied with master's degrees from other departments such as teacher education.

The seventh and final phase of the program had begun: dying. The neighbor island students remained enthusiastic about the opportunity to have access to graduate education from a remote location. However, increasing competition from other programs both from the College of Education and from external providers (such as Heritage College and University of Phoenix) meant that students had more choices, and enrollment dwindled slightly.

Bridges (2003) notes that at stage five it is possible to move toward organizational renewal. This involves decisions to redream the dream, recapture the venture spirit, and begin anew. There was now such an opportunity for the IMED program. The college hired a new outreach coordinator to work with neighbor island programs. He felt that IMED should continue its service through use of distance technology, offering all courses online. He purchased equipment for distance delivery and was eager to put it to use. However, the program's philosophy held that the pedagogically soundest way to deliver course content and create community was in-person. This sense of community, for the program's students and the faculty, was one of the fundamental values of the program. Although faculty members used technology as a last resort, they were skeptical about the ability of online courses to accomplish these goals and felt that this mode of course delivery violated one of their most closely held values. It was this clash of ideas, coupled with eroding support from the host department and the dean, that contributed to IMED's demise.

New Directions for Community Colleges • DOI: 10.1002/cc

The Ecology of the System

From an ecological perspective, Morgan (1998) explains that organizations need to be both aware and responsive to their external environments if they are to survive. Accordingly, the death of an organization is largely dependent on the organization's standing in its environment. Morgan suggests that an organization comprises numerous subsystems, which are interrelated for the organization to function adequately. These subsystems may include individuals, small team units, departments, colleges, and the institution as a whole. Subsystems must align with other subsystems in order to sustain themselves and the larger organizational unit. In this theory, if a subsystem does not align with the rest of the organization, it may be viewed as a potential dysfunction and eliminated. As the college expanded and became more technologically sophisticated, the IMED grew out of sync with the goals of the larger organization. Although it was never dysfunctional within itself, it came to be seen as a less vital part of the college's outreach initiatives.

Morgan (1998) points out that in organizational systems and subsystems "one element of this configuration always has important consequences for the other" (p. 40). As indicated earlier, the choices of particular technical systems have inevitable human consequences. IMED faculty members were concerned that social relationships among students and faculty would be compromised if they emphasized technology. When oversight for IMED shifted to the newly created outreach arm of the college, the pressure to teach fewer traditional courses and more technology-mediated ones began to grow. Some faculty members balked and refused to deliver their courses using any form of electronic media except email communication. Other faculty members who were more adept and experienced at distance technologies were open to the idea. However, the faculty as a collective argued that the strength of the program was in regular face-to-face contact. These opportunities helped to build professional networks and friendships that were sustained through working together, planning together, eating together, telling stories, coming early, staying late, and simply being in one another's presence. Indeed, actual (rather than virtual) "social presence" was a key cohesive factor. Although research indicates that social presence can be achieved with some success through electronic media (Leong, 2006), the faculty members who continued to work in the IMED program thrived in the culture precisely because they enjoyed being together and participating in a community of scholar and educators who were innovative and anxious to serve students in the remoter parts of the state.

The model that Morgan (1998) borrows from biology to describe human organizations has a number of aspects that apply to the IMED. His metaphor of organization as ecology allows us to tell the story of the program in a way that clarifies and illuminates certain aspects of its relationship to the environment in which it existed and to explain the patterns that led to eventual demise. In many ways, termination of the program was due to a range of environmental and internal factors that reflect larger problems in delivery of educational programs to remote areas. The language of open systems that Morgan employs also offers possibilities for explaining why the IMED was so successful in many dimensions and yet, despite its success, ceased to exist.

Our general analysis of the life and demise of the IMED program is followed by our impressionistic tales. Joanne, the program director for the entire ten years (except while on sabbatical), will begin. Her story is followed by Gay's, who served as the graduate chair for the program in the final rounds and stepped in as temporary co-director when Joanne was on sabbatical. Finally, Llewellyn gives his impressions from the perspective of an instructor and doctoral student who participated in the final round of the program.

Impressionist Tale One: Joanne

In the fall of 1995, the dean of the College of Education called to tell me that I was to teach a course in the new interdisciplinary master's program on the neighbor island of Kauai. I was startled. Why did no one tell me this was part of my load? Hesitant to tell the dean no, I said I would travel to Kauai on weekends and teach after I submitted my tenure papers in October. Thus my ten-year journey in IMED was born.

I met with faculty from six other programs and slowly began to understand the purpose of this effort to deliver graduate education to the neighbor islands. We had nineteen delightful students, mostly public school teachers on Kauai. We met each weekend at the community college on Kauai, which gave us classrooms, library support, and a general feeling of welcome. We got to know the staff and some faculty. It was a wonderful collaboration.

Shortly after the program began, we stumbled upon a major oversight on the part of the original planners. There was no one running this program. The dean had been involved in the original planning but was too busy to be involved in day-to-day operations. My colleague from Counseling and Guidance and I stepped into the void, agreeing to run the program jointly. We negotiated overload pay for ourselves as directors of the program and for the faculty who took on extra work in curricular design and advising.

I loved having a second home in the college, a strong community of scholars who talked on a regular basis about teaching and learning. We dreamed of innovative course structures, talked philosophies of teacher leadership, and asked the students to create a personal and professional development file that tracked their learning throughout the program. By the time our students were ready for graduation, they were reporting on their development through papers and presentations—and even quilts. It was curricular heaven for me. I could see that our dream of creating strong communities of learners was coming true. For example, students from the second cohort shared that they "learned way more from each other than we did from the faculty." This was true leadership on our part, to empower our students to this extent. It still makes me smile when I think about it.

NEW DIRECTIONS FOR COMMUNITY COLLEGES • DOI: 10.1002/cc

The program lost some faculty (my fellow director stepped down after the first round) and gained new enthusiastic recruits. Our meetings were characterized by laughter, costumes at Halloween, and, one Christmas, a spontaneous rendition of "Jingle Bells." This morphed into a version entitled "IMED Bells," which was sung for the students at graduation in 2006. Yet I began to feel an erosion of this enthusiasm as we moved into the fourth round of the program, which was split between Moloka'i and Kona, on the big island. The faculty members were being pulled between their duties in IMED and the demands of their home departments who were developing new master's programs of their own.

In fact, the Department of Educational Foundations developed a second master's degree in teacher leadership based partly on the model of IMED. When the new department chair began to see IMED as competition for this second teacher leadership degree, I worried about our program's future. When the college's new director of technology wanted to put the next round of the program entirely online, I worried about our commitment to creation of community. One faculty member said he was getting a lot of pressure to teach in his department's new master's program. When he said the only reason he was still with IMED was because he liked working with me, I felt both pleased and scared. I felt that I must be doing something right, but where were we all headed? The ground under my feet was crumbling, and I was getting tired. I felt like the woman who was holding up half the sky; when was it acceptable to let go? When was it wrong to hang on? Was I really facing the reality of the situation? Somewhere along this path, I decided the handwriting was on the wall. I couldn't ask faculty members to go on under these circumstances, even though I knew we were serving students well.

Impressionist Tale Two: Gay

Camaraderie and connectedness are the words that most aptly describe my experience of teaching in the IMED over a decade. I was one of the fortunate faculty members who began with the first round on Kauai, continued through two rounds on Maui, and ended with the Kona and Moloka'i cohort. The cohort model that brought students together into learning communities also brought faculty members from different departments into a deeply rewarding professional kinship. We shared a commitment to reaching underserved parts of the state, to innovative teaching and program development, to making deep and lasting connections with students, and to helping teachers create personal and professional networks of support that continued long after we completed the program.

Over time, we sought to make the program more integrated, to move it from multidisciplinary status toward a truly interdisciplinary model. The thematic approach with its focus on teacher leadership helped bring this about. But it was our attempts to play with the curriculum by responding to needs assessments, spreading courses over several semesters, developing a string course that focused on the concept of teacher leadership, and teaching two courses together with a joint project that moved the program toward greater interdisciplinarity.

Another personally gratifying aspect of the program was the gradual movement toward indigenization. Although several of us were *kamaʻaina* (long-term residents with special connection to Hawaiʻi), we were cultural outsiders. By the last round, we had two faculty members of native Hawaiian ancestry and one with deep local roots. The number of Native Hawaiian students also grew. It is difficult to quantify the sense of *ʻohana* (family) that emerges when Hawaiian culture is infused into a program. We began to feel a strong sense of place and rootedness that made the experience more profound. Indigenization came about partly because of being on Molokaʻi for half of the final round. In this rural, less commercial setting, we felt the power of the land and the culture more poignantly. These were some of the forces that brought us together as a cohesive unit of faculty and students.

From my perspective, there were several contributions to the demise of the program. As is often the case, the greatest strength is also the greatest weakness. The culture of the college more easily sustains programs that are taught by faculty in a single department. Interdisciplinarity is valued theoretically, but in actual implementation it gets bureaucratically messy and untenable. To really serve the unique needs of differing populations, flexible course content and program design were essential. The faculty worked around the bureaucracy to deliver a culturally relevant and meaningful educational experience.

In addition, the demise seemed to come about because of the homelessness mentioned earlier. Although the Foundations Department agreed to house the program, fewer foundations faculty taught in the program. At the same time, the department developed its own home-grown version of a teacher leadership program, and IMED came to be seen as a competitor. The pressure to teach in programs in our home department and to replace face-to-face instruction with online courses took a toll on the IMED.

For most of us, teaching on an overload basis was not a problem, but it became increasingly difficult to justify a program that had no designated faculty. We continued to work in IMED because of the satisfaction derived from working together, and we appreciated our unique status as an interdisciplinary program. We all deeply valued the face-to-face and context-sensitive approach and saw it as conducive to building strong learning communities. Travel to neighbor islands was crucial to understanding the contexts that our students worked in, but it was also time-consuming. Despite the warm reception from administrators at the community colleges and the gratitude of students who deeply appreciated our commitment to bring the program to them, it became clear by the fourth round that the IMED was on its last legs. There was a bitter sweetness in the final offering, when we tacitly knew that this would probably be the culmination of our work together. Thankfully, we have found ways to keep the connections

NEW DIRECTIONS FOR COMMUNITY COLLEGES • DOI: 10.1002/cc

alive beyond the demise of the program and have discovered new opportunities for creative collaboration.

Impressionist Tale Three: Llewellyn

In Hawai'i, the neighbor islands are often neglected when it comes to graduate education. Each has its own community college, but only two of the major islands house four-year public institutions. As a person of Native Hawaiian descent from the neighbor island of Kauai, I experienced these struggles personally and felt a responsibility to the neighbor islanders. My destiny was to become a faculty member of the IMED program.

I was also told that the faculty members teaching for IMED were a fantastic bunch of people. I knew most of the members in the group, and they were truly the most dedicated, professional, and knowledgeable professors in their fields. It was truly an honor to be a part of this team.

At my first IMED faculty meeting, I was in awe. The camaraderie between faculty members was extraordinary. The professors worked extremely well together to accomplish tasks, and subsequent meetings were no less productive. The atmosphere was always positive and focused on the learners. However, I sensed a subtle reluctance to afford the program any more than the minimal time required to ensure its success. Reasons for this reluctance included faculty having to work on overload to be a part of IMED, having no release time authorized for the program, and already having additional duties from their home departments.

Support for the IMED program from the college administration was also minimal. Although the program received sufficient funding for basic operations, I sensed a hesitation on the part of the administration to give IMED any additional resources. The reason stemmed from other departments who were offering services to the neighbor islands and providing more graduate education opportunities for educators. These programs were highly specialized compared with the interdisciplinary IMED program. Discussions at IMED faculty meetings often included topics on how the college administration was not fully supportive in securing IMED's future.

However, support from the IMED students and the cooperating community colleges on the neighbor islands was uncompromised. The IMED students were appreciative to be a part of such a worthwhile program. Class sessions were always stimulating and productive. Students commented on how they thought the IMED program filled a niche for neighbor islanders and that such a program should most definitely continue. The community colleges were also very supportive in allowing us to use their facilities and technological resources. The staff was quite accommodating and always helpful. Two IMED students were employed by the neighbor island community colleges; they believed that IMED opened doors to both K–12 and higher education educators and administrators in comparison to most other programs that targeted only K–12.

NEW DIRECTIONS FOR COMMUNITY COLLEGES • DOI: 10.1002/cc

On a more personal note, the program held a cultural meaning for me as a Native Hawaiian. On the neighbor islands, many residents form tight communities where the notion of family extends to persons who may not be related through bloodlines. Most of us born in the islands have extended "family" residing on other islands and therefore have a vested interest and duty in seeing others in these communities advance. During my first trip to Molokaʻi, a focus island during my involvement with IMED, a familial connection was made when I learned that all of the students knew my elderly godparents, who were prominent members of their community. Similar connections were made with some of the big-island students. In essence, we were one large extended family. Other IMED faculty members embraced the cultural customs of the islands and had connections of their own. These customs emphasized the importance of giving students the guidance and understanding to navigate the rigors of a graduate education and did not compromise our academic duties to challenge them. This learner-centered approach took priority, and professors strived to ensure that students grasped the concepts being presented. We all took pride in IMED, and hence it was emotional to see such a program come to an end, but there was satisfaction in knowing that this program touched the lives of many neighbor islanders and brought the opportunity of a quality graduate education to their doorstep.

Conclusions

Common threads run through our impressionist tales. We all agreed that the demise of the IMED was brought about by the changing ecology of the program. As the college expanded its many program offerings to remote parts of the state, the need for the IMED dwindled and the program was seen as competing with the newer offerings. Competition for instructor time and the push to more efficient delivery systems also had an impact. Bridges's life-cycle categories (2003) were an appropriate metaphor for our experience. All three of us felt the power and purpose of the IMED and the camaraderie that developed among the faculty. For Llewellyn and Gay, the cultural dimensions were particularly important; all three of us felt a sense of loss at the end of the final round when we knew there was no way to sustain the IMED within the host department and in the college's evolving system.

When we explore the dynamics of the program in terms of partnership, we agree that partnership with the community colleges was a constant that helped the program grow and flourish. The partnership among the seven departments was unprecedented at the graduate level and remains a model of interdisciplinarity in the college. Ultimately it is the human connections that define the outcomes. The IMED was a multifaceted partnership that grew the relationships among faculty, students, and colleges. In this respect the program was a success, even in its demise.

New Directions for Community Colleges • DOI: 10.1002/cc

References

Adizes, I. "The 10 Stages of Corporate Life Cycles." *Industrial Management,* 1996, *18*(14), 95–98.

Adizes, I. "Embrace One Problem After Another." *Industrial Management,* 2004, *46*(2), 18–25.

Bridges, W. *Managing Transitions: Making the Most of Change.* Cambridge, Mass.: Perseus, 2003.

Cooper, J., Brandon, P., and Lindberg, M. "Evaluator's Use of Peer Debriefing: Three Impressionist Tales." *Qualitative Inquiry,* 1998, *4*(2), 265–280.

Leong, P. "Understanding Interactivity in Online Learning Environments: The Role of Social Presence and Cognitive Absorption in Student Satisfaction with Online Courses." Unpublished doctoral dissertation, University of Hawai'i, 2006.

Morgan, G. *Images of Organization: The Executive Edition.* New York: Sage, 1998.

Van Maanen, J. *Tales of the Field: On Writing Ethnography.* Chicago: University of Chicago Press, 1988.

GAY GARLAND REED *is an associate professor in the College of Education at the University of Hawai'i.*

JOANNE E. COOPER *is a professor in the Department of Educational Administration at the University of Hawai'i.*

LLEWELLYN YOUNG *currently consults and develops curriculum for universities offering distance education.*

PART THREE

Other Perspectives on Educational Partnership

9

This chapter discusses collaboration associated with four public policies at the federal and state levels to show how partnerships are encouraged and how they struggle. The chapter concludes with lessons learned about the complex intersection between policy and practice.

The Legislative Playing Field: How Public Policy Influences Collaboration

Debra D. Bragg, Maxine L. Russman

Recognizing that lasting change is possible when organizations form a partnership, public policy increasingly drives active sharing of resources and mutual commitment to accountability and heightened productivity. Legislation that emphasizes aligning and improving the educational system; supporting the transition from high school to college and transfer between community college and university; and ensuring workforce, economic, and community development requires and reinforces the necessity for collaboration. This chapter defines collaboration and examines federal and state public policies to show how partnership is encouraged and how it can struggle. The chapter concludes with lessons learned from examining the complex intersection between policy and practice.

Collaboration Defined

The word *collaboration* is derived from the Latin *co-,* meaning together, and *laborare,* meaning work. Simply put, collaboration means to work together (Roberts and Bradley, 1991). Gray (1989) described collaboration as a process where "parties who see different aspects of a problem can constructively explore their differences and search for solutions that go beyond their own limited vision of what is possible" (p. 5). Himmelman (1996) defined organizational collaboration as "a process in which organizations exchange information, alter activities, share resources and enhance each other's capacity for

mutual benefit and a common purpose by sharing risks, responsibilities, and rewards" (p. 22).

Mattessich and Monsey (1992) conducted an extensive review of the literature and identified factors that influence the success of collaborations, grouping them into six categories: environment, membership, process and structure, communications, purpose, and resources. The *environment* category suggests that a history of collaboration and a favorable political and social climate are key factors in a partnership. Factors relating to the *membership* category include mutual respect, understanding, and trust. The *process* and *structure* category comprises members sharing a stake in processes and outcomes, and development of roles and policy guidelines that encourage and support adaptability. *Communication* refers to open and frequent informal and formal communication within the membership and with external stakeholders. *Purpose,* the fifth category, includes concrete, attainable goals and objectives, a shared vision, and unique purpose. The final category, *resources,* includes ensuring the collaboration has adequate funds to support its operations as well as a skilled convener, referring to an individual who convenes the group and ensures the members carry out their roles.

The Community College as a Collaborative Organization

Historically, community colleges have stressed the importance of community building through extended services associated with adult basic education (ABE) and the general educational development test (GED); workforce, economic, and community development; relationships with the K–12 sector; remedial and developmental education; incumbent and displaced worker training; and community education and development (Grubb and others, 1997). Community colleges often use collaboration to increase access and serve constituent needs, address competition and avoid duplication, and expand resources. For some community college leaders, collaboration is a vital strategy to ensure that the comprehensive mission of the community college is sustained, particularly when resources are limited or diminishing.

In 1980, the American Association of Community and Junior Colleges (AACJC) called for its one thousand member institutions to build a network of cooperation among organizations in the community to shape and sustain the comprehensive mission. Results of these forums identified three values held in high esteem by community colleges that engaged in collaborations: outreach is enhanced, learning opportunities are expanded beyond the traditional classroom, and the collaborative endeavor is attributed with increasing respect for the high social value of education. More than a decade after the AACJC's forum, the League for Innovation in the Community College (1993) declared that community colleges had made progress on collaboration. However, more is needed. The league observed that community colleges should emerge as "the nexus for the resolution of both local and national concerns" because they already serve as a "frequent hub for local networks dealing with community problems" (p. v).

Collaborative efforts assist community colleges in promoting access and serve their communities and local constituents in numerous ways. The role of the community college in collaboration ranges from minimal involvement to extensive leadership. On a minimal level, a community college can become involved in collaborative partnership by offering faculty expertise, physical space, or financial resources so other organizations can achieve their desired goals. At the other end of the spectrum, a community college can act as a catalyst for communitywide activities and programs tasked with leading social change. These complex, multilayered efforts can engage the community college as a partner in planning, implementing, and evaluating projects, programs, and activities over a sustained period.

Augustine and Rosevear (1998) conducted case studies of several collaborative relationships between community colleges and external constituents to investigate why colleges entered into collaborative partnership. They concluded that community colleges use collaboration as a tool to take advantage of market opportunities and limit or control environmental threats. They sometimes pursue structured collaboration that involves a signed agreement and formal administrative procedures as a strategy to increase their ability to compete in the new knowledge economy and to share the resources required to meet growing constituent needs. Federal and state legislation is often especially sensitive to competition and resource sharing as a primary reason of collaboration, as is illustrated by this discussion of two policies at the federal level and two at the state level.

Federal and State Policies and Practices

Federal and state policies and practices are playing an increasingly important role in encouraging community colleges to engage in collaborative partnership, influencing the organizations with whom community colleges partner and how they collaborate to better serve their students and communities.

Federal Policy and Practice. Through the federal Department of Labor and the Department of Education, the government has administered legislation that engages community colleges in central ways. Discussed here are two federal laws and how community colleges engage in collaborative partnership, specifically the Workforce Investment Act of 1998 and the Carl D. Perkins Career and Technical Education Improvement Act of 2006.

The Workforce Investment Act (WIA) of 1998 mandates that any entity receiving federal funds for adult education, literacy, and vocational education be an involved partner in a one-stop-center delivery system. One-stop centers are intended to provide an array of career-related programs and services and match job seekers (often displaced workers) to local employers. First funded by the U.S. Department of Labor in 1995, one-stop delivery systems were envisioned as a means of addressing the fragmentation of existing employment and training systems.

From the beginning, federally funded employment training agencies were mandated partners in one-stop centers; elective partners included community colleges and other community-based organizations. Because many community colleges receive federal WIA funds, they are required to commit to one-stop delivery systems as a means of serving local workforce development initiatives and contributing to the training of individual citizens. Kogan and others (1997) pointed out that one-stop delivery systems do not happen without careful attention to detail because individual partners are tied to categorical funding streams, each with its own target population, eligibility criteria, reporting requirements, and performance standards. To overcome barriers associated with turf, successful one-stop career centers ensure clear guidelines, productive communication processes, and shared outcomes among all partners, including the community college.

Russman (2001) studied the community college role in one-stop delivery systems from the vantage point of the leader who is designated as a collaborative agent. This term refers to an individual with formal connections to an organization who is accountable to that organization and who is also actively engaged in leading the collaborative process with community partners. A community college collaborative agent has the challenging job of balancing and integrating the interests of the community college with those of other partners. Collaborative agents operate fundamentally differently from traditional leaders in that they often have no formal authority and recognized, agreed-on rules and procedures (Gershwin, 1999). Russman's study showed collaborative agents play a critical role in ensuring that one-stop centers work effectively from the standpoint of the community college. They are expected to "balance opposites" (p. 156) by encouraging new collaborative endeavors to meet partner needs while also protecting the community college's core mission. They are rewarded by their community college executive leaders for building on past history and maintaining long-term relationships with partners. When difficulties with collaboration emerge, it is often because the partners lose sight of a one-stop center's collective goals and the collaborative agent is unable to maintain the balance needed to sustain the partner organization's commitment.

The Carl D. Perkins Career and Technical Education Improvement Act of 2006 supports career and technical education programs by encouraging student transition to college and entry into careers, and by promoting curriculum linkages to career pathways (Hull, 2005). Schwartz (2004) situated career pathways within a larger debate about high school reform as a means of enhancing college access, affirming the need for multiple pathways to prepare more high school students to matriculate to college. On behalf of the League for Innovation in the Community College, Warford (2006) defines *career pathways* as a "coherent, articulated sequence of rigorous academic and career courses, commencing in the ninth grade and leading to an associate degree, and (or) an industry-recognized certificate or licensure, and (or) a baccalaureate degree and beyond. A career pathway is developed, implemented, and maintained in partnership among secondary and postsecondary education, business, and employers. Career pathways are available to all students, including adult learners, and are designed to lead to rewarding careers" (p. 8).

Implementation of a career pathway requires collaborative relationships among secondary schools, community colleges, and four-year colleges and universities. In addition, business and industry and community-based organizations partner with community colleges and high schools in offering curriculum aligned with academic and occupational standards. Career pathway programs are expected to offer multiple entry and exit points leading to viable employment, business, and entrepreneurial opportunities. The programs are encouraged to award college credit through credit-based transition programs such as dual credit, dual enrollment, and tech prep, ensuring academic preparation consistent with students being college-ready on entry to the postsecondary level.

Indicative of the collaborative partnerships that undergird career pathways, the College and Careers Transition Initiative (CCTI) of the League for Innovation in the Community College is designed to assist community colleges and local partner organizations to implement career pathways (Warford, 2006). Using federal funding from the Office of Vocational and Adult Education, the league formed a leadership team and invited partner organizations such as the American Association of Community Colleges (AACC) to furnish technical assistance. Fifteen community college–led partnerships were selected using a competitive process, each being tasked with forming a local consortium-type organization. Collaborative CCTI partnerships are charged formally with coordinating activities, communicating actively, collecting qualitative and quantitative data, and using these data to improve programs. Three partnerships were selected for each of the five career cluster areas of education and training; health science; information technology; law, public safety, and security; and science, technology, engineering, and mathematics.

Positive outcomes associated with creation of the CCTI community college–led partnerships include development of shared decision-making processes for partner institutions, frequent communication of goals and strategies to encourage and support buy-in by key partners, and creation of seamless career pathway curriculum and support services dedicated to student success (Warford, 2006). Among the challenges to collaboration are difficulty in gauging the scope of the initiative and the potential contributions from partner institutions; problems with sharing resources, particularly when governmental guidelines limit how funds can be used and by whom; difficulty in knowing when organizations should cooperate and when they should maintain autonomy; and inadequacy in developing and sustaining the data collection systems needed to measure student and program success.

State Policy and Practice

On the state level, two policies that promote collaboration are examined; particular attention is paid to the role of the community college as collaborative organization. These two policies are the Illinois Articulation Initiative and the Community College P–16 Accelerated College Enrollment grant program. Even though these two initiatives are specific to Illinois, they offer valuable examples of collaborations that occur within states throughout the country.

In 1992, the idea of the Illinois Articulation Initiative (IAI) was first introduced to the state by the Illinois Board of Higher Education (IBHE). The IAI is a voluntary statewide transfer agreement involving more than one hundred two-year and four-year public and independent institutions in the state. Kelly and Lach (2006) pointed out that IAI was an outgrowth of the state's desire to improve undergraduate education and increase opportunities for minority and low-income students to transfer. From its inception, the IAI was designed to facilitate transfer of courses between two-year and four-year colleges and universities; enhance time-to-degree; and promote student opportunities to attain collegiate-level knowledge, skills, and credentials, including the bachelor's degree (Kelly and Lach, 2006).

In 1994, faculty panels began work on articulating general education subject areas, and in 1995 the state's first curriculum recommendations were adopted in two major fields: engineering and nursing. Development of course descriptions has continued in general education and major subject matter fields since the mid-1990s. Transfer from community colleges to universities is an important but not exclusive focus; IAI recognizes that transfer occurs in multiple ways (upward, laterally, and downward) among higher education institutions. IAI has had a substantial impact on the state's transfer enterprise, as evidenced by the fact that transfer agreements are now in place in twenty-seven major fields, with guidance provided to students, parents, and college and university faculty and advisors through the itransfer Website (http://www.itransfer.org).

Collaboration is extremely important to the success of IAI. Communication of expectations of content and quality standards pertaining to transfer of course work is essential for IAI to achieve its goal of transferring students who are prepared academically to transfer and capable of achieving degree completion. Sack (2006) observed that collaboration among colleges and universities in implementation of IAI benefits the educational institutions as well as their students. Voluntary compliance is an important aspect of IAI, seeking cooperation and commitment from higher education institutions and their employees—especially faculty—to carry out the difficult work of developing course agreements that is necessary to make IAI work.

Despite documented accomplishments, IAI has experienced challenges to the collaborative relationships among two-year and four-year institutions (Kelly and Lach, 2006; Sack, 2006). Faculty at a number of levels demonstrated varying support for participation in the IAI panels, sometimes reflecting the nature of commitment from their parent organization. Concerns with commitment to IAI have been noted by the state's flagship university wherein faculty and administrators lament that IAI has not increased course content standards as anticipated at its inception. These concerns are reflective of the dominance of four-year institutions that Ignash (1992) found in the transfer literature more than a decade ago, suggesting a continuing challenge to realizing that two-year and four-year institutions are partners that, though different, in many respects make contributions of equal importance to the overall educational system.

Paralleling the commitment to transferring students within higher education, the state shows a strong commitment to transitioning students successfully from high school to college. Indicative of this commitment, the state's initiative to support high-school-to-college transition is called the Community College P–16 Accelerated Learning Opportunity grant program. In Illinois, dual-credit programs are guided and monitored by the Illinois Community College Board, with support from the state's K–12 agency, the Illinois State Board of Education, and the Illinois Board of Higher Education.

Dual-enrollment programs have grown significantly throughout the state. Between 2000 and 2004, enrollment jumped from six thousand to thirty-six thousand. Part of the reason is the availability of Community College P–16 Accelerated Learning Opportunity grants that support all or part of the college tuition and fees for participating high school students. As such, high schools do not experience the financial burden of losing students because resources are awarded on both levels. With this approach, two-year and four-year colleges have adequate resources to enroll additional students and support increased instructional costs. Referred to as "double dipping" (recall the discussion in Chapter Seven), this financial model has helped advance dual credit in the state of Illinois by removing finances as a major stumbling block to collaboration among secondary and postsecondary partners (Vargas, 2004).

Implementation of dual-credit courses and programs requires collaboration among secondary and postsecondary institutions and their administrators, faculty, and advising and counseling staff. Rasch (2002) studied collaborations associated with dual credit and found that state-level P–16 goals were met through improved communication among secondary and postsecondary institutions, resulting in enhanced curriculum alignment. Collaborative activities undertaken by community colleges and other partners include assessing student knowledge and skills, enrolling secondary students in college-level courses and tracking their progress and performance, and working on transfer and articulation agreements to ensure students can continue their education at four-year colleges and universities. As one example, Rash noted that Illinois community colleges have developed teacher preparation models that give students a full two years of teacher preparation at the community college without losing credits at the baccalaureate level. To help more students matriculate to the university level, several community colleges and four-year universities developed agreements that allow associate degree students to remain on the community college campus to finish the bachelor's degree.

Like other policy-driven endeavors, collaboration among educational institutions is vital to the success of dual-credit and other accelerated learning opportunity programs. Working with a state-level task force on dual-credit policy, Kim, Barnett, and Bragg (2003) identified issues surrounding coordination between levels, notably lack of clarity about leader responsibilities to the collaboration. They observed that good communication is needed between administrators at the secondary and postsecondary levels. Barnett, Gardner, and Bragg (2004) identified these same concerns, adding that program development is enhanced with use of management systems; standard forms for student admissions; and consistent policies dealing with class scheduling, course withdrawal, placement testing, and reporting to parents on student progress. Studying collaboration on dual credit with Illinois's four-year universities, Makela (2005) showed that, despite the strong commitment of a growing number of high schools and community colleges to dual credit and a desire among many of the state's four-year universities to award dual credit, lack of adequate information pervades the four-year college and university level. She advised the state to develop policies and practices that communicate clearly about dual credit to all levels of the educational system and to all constituents, especially students and parents.

Lessons Learned

Analysis of the four federal and state policies demonstrates how expectations for collaboration among educational institutions, including community colleges, are evolving. To summarize, we look again at the six categories of factors influencing the success of collaboration as identified by Mattessich and Monsey (1992), and we consider the selected legislation in light of this framework. Table 9.1 presents results of our analysis of the four policies across the six categories, displaying an X in boxes where the extant research, some of our own and some by others, shows an important alignment.

Our analysis shows environment is an important factor associated with all four pieces of legislation. Drawing on historical developments, the collaborations associated with the four policies were influenced by events that preceded them. Where partners had built on past successes, present efforts at collaboration were enhanced because of the favorable rapport already established. Our analysis of the policies also suggested collaboration did not always engage educational organizations that considered each other with

Table 9.1. How Four Federal and State Policies Align with Factors Influencing the Success of Collaboration.

Factors Influencing the Success of Collaboration	Federal WIA Policy	Federal Career and Technical Education Policy	State Transfer Policy	State Dual Credit Policy
Environment	X	X	X	X
Membership	X	X		
Process/ Structure	X	X	X	X
Communication	X	X	X	X
Purpose	X	X		X
Resources		X	X	X

Source: Mattessich and Monsey (1992).

mutual respect. Difficulties with articulation and transfer policies created by a sense of unequal status and inequitable resources diminished the collaborative endeavors associated with the IAI, and to some extent the state's efforts to implement dual credit. In cases where processes and structures were put into place to support collaboration, we observed that collaborative endeavors benefited. Partnerships between state agencies and among local educational organizations were stimulated and sustained when a clear set of guidelines, procedures, and outcomes were established and followed.

Our review of the four policies on the dimension of communication showed the vital importance of clear, accurate, ongoing communication among individuals representing the partnering organizations. In cases where communication broke down, collaborative endeavors struggled. Whenever active communication occurred, the partnerships operated successfully. A shared purpose, the fifth category, was evident in three of the four policies. Where purpose was not clearly defined in terms of common goals and values and a shared vision, specifically with respect to some aspects of transferring courses with the IAI, the collaboration suffered. Finally, resources that were put toward the common good and used to fulfill shared goals were critical to the success of collaboration. In all cases except the WIA, we saw a shared commitment of resources that encouraged partnership and cooperative behavior (though we recognize this finding may not be true universally and therefore caution about too liberal a generalization). Specifically with WIA, distinctive funding streams support related (but sometimes competing or uncooperative) organizational behaviors. Yet on the local level, one-stop delivery systems can operate entirely collaboratively, if the commitment of local collaborative agents creates the all-important balance that is required to meet organizational expectations and serve client needs.

NEW DIRECTIONS FOR COMMUNITY COLLEGES • DOI: 10.1002/cc

References

Augustine, C., and Rosevear, S. "Looking Outward: Changing Organizations Through Collaboration." *Community College Journal of Research and Practice,* 1998, 22(3), 419–433.

Barnett, E., Gardner, D., and Bragg, D. *Dual Credit in Illinois: Making It Work.* Champaign: Office of Community College Research and Leadership, University of Illinois at Urbana-Champaign, 2004.

Gershwin, M. C. "Collaborating on Behalf of the Organization: Lessons from Inter Organizational Agents." Unpublished doctoral dissertation, University of Denver, 1999.

Gray, B. *Collaborating: Finding Common Ground for Multiparty Problems.* San Francisco: Jossey-Bass, 1989.

Grubb, W. N., Badway, N., Bell, D., Bragg, D., and Russman, M. *Workforce, Economic, and Community Development: The Changing Landscape of the Entrepreneurial Community College.* Mission Viejo, Calif.: League for Innovation in the Community College, 1997.

Himmelman, A. T. "Rationales and Context for Collaboration." In C. Huxham (ed.), *Creating Collaboration Advantage.* London: Sage, 1996.

Hull, D. "Career Pathways: Education with a Purpose." In D. Hull (ed.), *Career Pathways: Education with a Purpose.* Waco, Tex.: Center for Occupational Research and Development, 2005.

Ignash, J. *In the Shadow of Baccalaureate Institutions.* Los Angeles: ERIC Clearinghouse for Junior Colleges, University of California, Los Angeles, 1992. (ED 348 129)

Kelly, K. F., and Lach, I. J. *Evaluation of the Illinois Articulation Initiative Report and Results.* Springfield: Illinois Board of Higher Education, 2006.

Kim, J., Barnett, E., and Bragg, D. *Dual Credit in Illinois: Results of Expert Panel Deliberations and a Delphi Study of Definitions and Priorities.* Champaign: Office of Community College Research and Leadership, University of Illinois at Urbana-Champaign, 2003.

Kogan, D., Dickinson, K. P., Redrau, R., Midling, J. J., and Wolff, K. E. *Creating Workforce Development Systems That Work: An Evaluation of the Initial One-Stop Implementation Experiences.* Washington, D.C.: U.S. Department of Labor, 1997.

League for Innovation in the Community College. *Catalysts for Community College Change: Guidelines for Community Colleges to Conduct Community Forums.* Mission Viejo, Calif.: League for Innovation in the Community College, 1993.

Makela, J. P. *Current Practices and Policies on Dual Credit Admissions in Illinois' Four-Year Colleges and Universities.* Champaign: Office of Community College Research and Leadership, University of Illinois at Urbana-Champaign, 2005.

Mattessich, P. W., and Monsey, B. R. *Collaboration: What Makes It Work?* St. Paul, Minn.: Amherst H. Wilder Foundation, 1992.

Rasch, E. *The Influence of State Policies on Community College Dual Credit Programs.* Champaign: Office of Community College Research and Leadership, University of Illinois at Urbana-Champaign, 2002.

Roberts, N. C., and Bradley, R. T. "Stakeholder Collaboration and Innovation: A Study of Public Policy Initiation at the State Level." *Journal of Applied Behavior Science,* 1991, 27(2), 209–227.

Russman, M. A. "Community College and One-Stop Center Collaboration: The Role of Community College Collaborative Agents." Unpublished doctoral dissertation, University of Illinois at Urbana-Champaign, 2001.

Sack, J. "Is IAI Improving Transfer?" *Update Newsletter,* 2006, 18(1), 12–15 (http://occrl.ed.uiuc.edu/Newsletter/2006/fall/UPDATEFall06.pdf; accessed Jun. 1, 2007).

Schwartz, R. B. "Multiple Pathways—and How to Get There." In R. Kazis, J. Vargas, and N. Hoffman (eds.), *Double the Numbers: Increasing Postsecondary Credentials for Underrepresented Youth.* Cambridge, Mass.: Harvard University Press, 2004.

Vargas, J. "Dual Enrollment: Lessons from Washington and Texas." In R. Kazis, J. Vargas, and N. Hoffman (eds.), *Double the Numbers: Increasing Postsecondary Credentials for Underrepresented Youths.* Cambridge, Mass.: Harvard University Press, 2004.

Warford, L. J. "College and Career Transitions Initiative: Responding to a Quiet Crisis." In L. J. Warford (ed.), *Pathways to Student Success: Case Studies from the College and Careers Transitions Initiative.* Phoenix, Ariz.: League for Innovation in the Community College, 2006.

DEBRA D. BRAGG is a professor of higher education and director of the Office of Community College Research and Leadership at the University of Illinois at Urbana-Champaign.

MAXINE L. RUSSMAN is an educational consultant for the Rock Island Regional Educational Office in Illinois.

10

This chapter revisits the partnerships described in this volume using the model outlined in Chapter One and introducing social and organizational capital as a largely ignored factor in the development and sustainability of partnerships.

Strategies for the Future

C. Casey Ozaki, Marilyn J. Amey, Jesse S. Watson

In Chapter One, we proposed a model outlining development of partnerships from initial conditions and motivations through the junction where the partnership must decide to adjust and preserve sustainability or end because the collaboration has fulfilled its goals or is no longer tenable. In this chapter, we illustrate how the case studies from this volume illuminate aspects of the model. We also propose adding social and organizational capital to the original model in Chapter One, suggesting these are two critical elements that have not been sufficiently explored. Finally, we offer suggestions for how administrators and policy makers can use the information from this volume to strategize for and appropriately encourage collaboration and partnership between postsecondary institutions.

The Model's Application to the Case Studies

The case studies presented in this volume demonstrate unique, contrasting, and complex processes of collaboration and varying degrees of success in their endeavors. The range of internal and external factors coupled with individual personalities and changing environments combine to create myriad partnerships, some of which are more sustainable and successful in achieving their goals than others. Viewing the case examples through the lens of our multidimensional model demonstrates the important aspects of the partnership development process and illuminates how collaboration depends on context and environment.

In these case studies, a range of antecedents prompted initiation of a partnership. Many of the collaborations occurred in a state climate that placed pressure on community colleges. Recall, for example, that colleges experienced increasing pressure to improve college attendance in Watson's Chapter Five. Economic concerns also contributed to collaboration; both Hoffman-Johnson's Chapter Two and Eddy's Chapter Six cases indicated that state and local economic challenges prompted the partnership. Additionally, Kisker and Hauser (Chapter Three) and Reed, Cooper, and Young (Chapter Eight) discussed the college mission as an antecedent. Finally, environment and contextual factors contribute to the shape and governance of the partnership itself (Jones, Hesterly, and Borgatti, 1997). For example, mandated collaborations seem to elicit contractual and formal structures to meet goals and expectations that can be more readily assessed and documented. In another example, the mission to serve the community and student needs led those in Kisker and Hauser's study (Chapter Three) to not only partner with local agencies on curriculum development and instruction but invite community members to serve on a departmental advisory board.

The antecedents identified in the preceding section are contextual challenges, changes, and characteristics that predate the institutions' desire to partner but also contribute to and serve as motivation and reason to collaborate. Yet throughout these cases, there are examples of institutions having their own reasons for partnering and situations where motivation to collaborate changed over time, affecting the trajectory of the partnership. For example, both Reed, Cooper, and Young's (Chapter Eight) and Eddy's (Chapter Six) cases demonstrated how changes in context—or even the expectations of the partnership—affect partners' motivation to continue in the collaboration. In Reed, Cooper, and Young's case, the cumulative effect of faculty changing over time, development of competing programs, and expansion of the college to remoter parts of the state resulted in less need and overall support for the program. Another example of changes negatively affecting a partnership is in Eddy's discussion of the Connected Campuses of Technology. Once the external imminent threat of institutional closure was gone, the original funding was spent, and CCT moved from a voluntary to mandatory partnership, the original reasons for banding together were gone and the alliance become a burden. Conversely, Kisker and Hauser's Chapter Three and Hoffman-Johnson's Chapter Two on program partnership demonstrated that the partnership is more likely to adjust to internal and external changes if governance and partnership structures are constructed with longevity, flexibility, and a shared mission.

In the first chapter, we identified two important aspects of partnership evolution: feedback and the champion. In the case studies of this volume, both factors prove critical to the sustainability or dissolution of the partnership. First, the presence of a champion and his or her ability to gather resources and support for the collaborative effort affects how the partnership develops and whether or not it can adjust for ongoing sustainability. In Hoffman-Johnson's (Chapter Two) and Watson's (Chapter Five) examples, the champions framed the potential partnership so as to gain necessary support from positional leaders and important stakeholders, as well as buy-in within the organizations in preparation for institutionalization. In Watson's case, the superintendent and community college administrator were both champions, but the analysis illustrated how they had their own social and organizational capital to draw on in order to develop the partnership. As a result, they managed sense making differently within their institutions in order to develop support. However, the collaboration remains possible because the champions can negotiate the specifics of the partnership with the resources and capital at their disposal. The organizational consultant in Hoffman-Johnson's case serves as champion by drawing on his reputation and organizational and social capital at each institution to broker the partnership. Although he does not hold a permanent position at either institution, he has enough support and resources to successfully initiate and structure the collaboration.

Conversely, Eddy's Chapter Six illustrates how lack of a champion for the partnership contributed to eventual breakdown of the alliance. Without a champion to help structure the partnership and broker rules among the colleges, there are few internal regulations keeping individual institutions from operating outside group norms. When an executive director was brought into the partnership, he did not have sufficient capital among the institutions or within the alliance to make a difference. Similarly, Reed, Cooper and Young (Chapter Eight) show the limits of champions who do not retain requisite capital in the face of changing environmental pressures. In spite of strong enthusiasm and commitment on the part of a dedicated team of instructors and students, shifting priorities and resources within the larger college setting eventually eroded the ability to sustain the partnership. Having not been fully institutionalized into the fabric of the department or college, the partnership was subject to the decisions of others who were in greater control of resources and, in this case, not fully behind the future of the collaboration.

Finally, the importance of paths for and integration of feedback is emphasized across the cases. The more successful or sustainable cases, such as Farrell and Seifert's (Chapter Seven) and Kisker and Hauser's (Chapter Three), are those that originally included feedback structures in the partnership (a departmental advisory board) and used them or eventually made adjustments on the basis of feedback. At times, hearing and integrating feedback means acknowledging the final, but natural, ending to the collaboration. Reed, Cooper, and Young's (Chapter Eight) recounting of the ten-year lifespan of the Interdisciplinary Master in Education program demonstrated how IMED originally served an important goal of affording access to graduate education for remote parts of the state, the need for which diminished as more graduate opportunities became available. Finally, Eddy's study (Chapter Six) of the technology campus partnership illustrated how lack of feedback loops aggravated unequal power distribution among colleges and poor communication, which together contributed to the eventual ending of the alliance.

Our model offers a heuristic for understanding not only what happened in the individual cases but why the collaborations developed as they did. Yet even though the model has been helpful, we noticed that it fell short in explaining important mechanisms in the development process. It became clear that many of the more successful and long-term collaborations had a champion with access to resources that were not necessarily tangible or easily developed and given. The ability to draw on reputation, relationships, and power within the college and sometimes outside it as well assisted champions in facilitating partnership development and meeting institutional goals. Specifically, the amount of and access to social and organizational capital seemed important pieces of the puzzle.

Social and Organizational Capital

Most resources critical to the development and ongoing operation of partnerships are concrete and tangible (funding, space, staff, supplies, time). But rarely do we acknowledge the role that a person's social and organizational capital plays in the ability to develop and establish a partnership. If multiple forms of capital are important for developing and sustaining partnerships but not readily acknowledged, we risk ignoring a critical element in the strategy of developing collaborations.

Social capital as a phenomenon was first identified in the sociological literature. The phrase refers to use of relationships or networks to facilitate action or obtain other resources of value. Social capital makes it possible to achieve certain goals when, in its absence, they would otherwise be impossible. Unlike other forms of capital, social capital exists in the structure of relationships between and among actors (Coleman, 1988). Important aspects within social capital that affect partnerships are reciprocity, trustworthiness, location, and time sensitivity. As a result, individuals involved in collaboration bring varying levels of capital to the table.

Recognized as a source of social capital, accumulation of obligations from others is more widely identified as the norm of reciprocity. Reciprocity is established when an actor provides "privileged access to resources in the expectation that they will be fully repaid in the future" (Portes, 1998, p. 7). This debt is not necessarily financial (it could be approval, access, or support) and may be repaid in a currency different from that in which it was originally given. Also, it generally does not have a time limit attached to it (Coleman, 1994; Portes, 1998).

Trustworthiness depends on the obligations that exist within the relationship and the extent to which they are repaid. A high number and usefulness of obligations at a given time results in more trustworthiness. Furthermore, as obligations are repaid and met within relationships, trustworthiness increases. Relational trustworthiness draws heavily on social capital (Coleman, 1988) and consists of a hierarchical relationship: one person must express trust before the other can respond with respect, competence, and integrity. If these properties are present, there is higher relational trust and, more likely, desired outcomes (Bryk and Schneider, 2002).

Another aspect of social capital—*location*—speaks to the connection of players within their social network to influential resources or people with access to resources such as information, authority, and decision-making influence. *Density* refers to the closeness or strength of these relationships, which helps understand location as an aspect of social capital (Granovetter, 1983). The stronger and closer the relationship, the more trustworthiness there will be in the beginning of the relationship. Partners are also likely to be more flexible with one another and persist through difficulty. Location has the ability to facilitate access to resources in social relationships and therefore helps to explain inequitable access. Finally, *time sensitivity* suggests that the longer the relationship, the stronger it is likely to be (Coleman, 1988). Density, intensity, trustworthiness, and extent of relationship networks determine the strength and amount of social capital available for productive ends.

Much like social capital, organizational capital is used to facilitate or achieve particular partnership goals for institutions. Unlike social capital, organizational capital is not limited to social structures and relationships, though it may include them. Rather, it takes many forms, ranging from cultural capital to formal structures and tangible resources. Furthermore, the resources, power, influence, authority, communication systems, and other aspects of the organization that individuals or a collective can draw on are unevenly distributed and may change over time (Kotter, 1996; Weick, 2001). Organizational capital may accrue or be tied to formal position, or it may be a function of other less tangible aspects of the organization such as years of institutional experience, expertise, and networks. For various reasons, the members of a partnership may be more or less able to use their social and organizational capital at a given point, thereby adding a dynamic feature to understanding how partnerships develop and are sustained or ended.

The literature on higher education institutional collaborations and partnerships is somewhat limited. Therefore, scholarship discussing the roles of social and organizational capital is even more scant. In contrast, the organizational behavior and business literatures extensively present how social and organizational capital influences the development and sustainability of networks, partnerships, and collaborations in the private sector. Although businesses are generally more competitive and have forms of exchange different from those of postsecondary institutions that serve a more altruistic mission, some general findings from this parallel literature can be applied to the development of collaboration in higher education.

First, social and organizational capital is critical at the beginning of the partnership (Todeva and Knoke, 2005). Who you know can serve as the impetus and starting point for collaboration. For example, in the case that Watson describes, the superintendent and community college representative were brought together through a third party who happened to be on a committee with one of them. Individual and institutional reputations, as forms of social capital, are also important for building trust early in the partnership. Factors such as available resources, trustworthiness for follow through, and genuineness of mission and goals have an impact on whether prospective partners want to become tied together in collaborative arrangements and are assessed on some level before even entering into relationships (Chung, Singh, and Lee, 2000). The two presidents in Hoffman-Johnson's case knew each other well enough to partner and agreed on an outside consultant to bring onto the project whose reputation with community colleges, the community, and the discipline was well known. These early assessments of social and organizational capital are not as easy with a partnership mandated by external agencies or state or federal policies, as noted in Farrell and Seifert (Chapter Seven) and Bragg and Russman (Chapter Nine). In these cases, motivation and willingness to trust in potentially risky initiatives may be inhibited. The amount of social or organizational capital that individuals have within a negotiated relationship, including an educational partnership, influences the degree to which individuals are supported by their own institutions, if they feel a level of tension and willingness to negotiate, and how informal or formal they wish the collaboration to be (Gray, 1989).

What often begins with a formal process (contracts) increasingly relies on social process (trust) as the partnership progresses and becomes more institutionalized. As the relational trust between individuals within the partnership grows, the rigidity of a formal partnership of a contract gives way to a more informal and flexible working relationship that is more likely to weather the need for ongoing negotiation and changes over time (Todeva and Knoke, 2005). Development of trust and the partnership are mutually reinforcing and circular. Movement from formal to social processes is dependent on development of trust, and as the partnership institutionalizes development of trust and reliance on relational capital contributes to flexibility and "learning."

Social and Organizational Capital Within the Case Studies

Examples from the cases demonstrate that social and organizational capital is instrumental in the inception and institutionalization phases of partnership development to a much greater extent than the higher education literature suggests.

Watson (Chapter Five) shows how social networks led to a meeting of the champions and their eventual collaboration. In addition, the superintendent and community college administrator brought differing levels of organizational and social capital to the partnership. Organizationally, the superintendent's position allowed him to make decisions about resources and participation almost unilaterally, so long as he could effectively frame the partnership for stakeholders. Conversely, as a midmanager the community college administrator had passion for the project. Although he did not have the positional power to independently enter and negotiate the partnership, he had enough organizational and social capital to garner the necessary support to move forward. Depending on the differences and mismatch of intent, purpose, and vision between the partners, the champion's capital can be drawn on to overcome and work through those issues.

The organizational consultant in Hoffman-Johnson's case (Chapter Two) is another example of how social and organizational capital facilitated the inception of a partnership. In lieu of formal positional power at either institution, the consultant's reputation, demonstrated accomplishments, professional network, and authority bestowed on him by the presidents generated enough capital to successfully broker the collaboration.

From Kisker and Hauser's description in Chapter Three of partnerships between an academic department and community agencies, one sees products of the ongoing collaboration (greater trust, investment of finances and time in the program by multiple stakeholders, more flexibility) contributing to its sustainability. Through invitation for community partners to sit on advisory panels, co-construct the mission statement for the program, and engage in mutually beneficial transactions, individual and organizational relationships are further emphasized. Relying on one another and following through helps partners develop trust, which encourages them to be more flexible and adjust in response to feedback.

Finally, Eddy (Chapter Six) shows what happens when some partners have more organization and capital than others. The organizational capital of each president's institution equated to power and capital within the coalition. Brought in to manage the coalition, the executive director did not have enough social or organizational capital to effectively make changes or manage it. Finally, because trust was not developed in the initial phases, norms that created and instilled loyalty—and repercussions for acting outside the norms—were never developed.

In addition to the components of our partnership development model described in Chapter One, we initially suggested that champions and feedback were factors affecting all phases and processes of development. From the experiences of the partnerships presented in this volume, we now also suggest that social and organizational capital is a third important factor. These forms of capital serve as a critical mechanism for partnership development, contributing to initiation and institutionalization of collaboration.

Policy Suggestions

Public and institutional policy makers tend to assume that a successful or good collaboration is a product of sufficient tangible resources, space, time, money, staff, and buy-in. In reality, we have found that champions, feedback, and social and organizational capital are also key considerations in partnership success. Social and organizational capital often serves as the impetus for beginning a partnership, influences the shape and overall governance of the collaboration, and acts as the glue that helps to cohere or break apart other factors in partnership evolution. Here are suggestions for administrators and policy makers derived from the case studies in this volume and our own analysis:

- All the institutions involved need to develop a long-term view of partnership beyond mandates.
- The partnership must create feedback loops and plans for how such feedback will be addressed. Developing relationships and effective communication is critical for this to occur.
- The champion not only leads but frames the collaboration for others. Therefore, the champion is a key facilitator of understanding in order to garner support.
- Successful partnerships have a champion with sufficient social and organizational capital to draw on and compensate for any potential lack of formal authority.
- Unequal distribution of social and organizational capital does not necessarily condemn a new partnership, but parties should be aware of the limitations and know how to compensate in these circumstances.
- Ongoing and institutionalized partnerships require time and much renegotiation.
- Mandated partnerships can backfire; institutional level buy-in is critical to the life of the collaboration.

Conclusion

The partnership model, complete with the addition of social and organizational capital, serves as a heuristic for developing better understanding of collaboration among postsecondary institutions. It draws attention to critical factors that exist in the development and operation of partnerships but that combine in diverse ways depending on the internal and external context leading to differential outcomes. The factor of our model that has largely been ignored in the higher education literature is social and organizational capital. Partnership development is facilitated when champions draw on and manage the capital available to them to create buy-in among stakeholders within their institutions and negotiate the terms of the collaboration and its evolution over time.

Policy makers who promote or discourage cross-institutional partnerships need to be made aware of the largely invisible but critical elements that have an impact on the outcomes and sustainability of the collaboration. It is often assumed that if there is a leader; if tangible resources are to found; and if a clear, shared motivation (mandated or voluntary) is present, the sum of these parts results in a good, lasting partnership. Consequently, when such a partnership ends seemingly without good reason, policy makers, administrators, and researchers are left perplexed. Yet what is often not taken into account is how organizational and social capital facilitate and shape the structure and governance of a partnership, thereby affecting its sustainability.

References

Bryk, A. S., and Schneider, B. L. *Trust in Schools: A Core Resource for Improvement.* New York: Russell Sage Foundation, 2002.

Chung, S., Singh, H., and Lee, K. "Complementarity, Status Similarity, and Social Capital as Drivers of Alliance Formation." *Strategic Management Journal,* 2000, *21,* 1–22.

Coleman, J. S. "Social Capital in the Creation of Human Capital." *American Journal of Sociology,* 1988, *94,* S95–S120.

Coleman, J. S. "The Realization of Effective Norms." In R. Collins (ed.), *Four Sociological Traditions: Selected Readings.* New York: Oxford University Press, 1994.

Granovetter, M. "The Strength of Weak Ties: A Network Theory Revisited." *Sociology Theory,* 1983, *1,* 201–233.

Gray, B. *Collaborating: Finding Common Ground for Multiparty Problems.* San Francisco: Jossey-Bass, 1989.

Jones, C., Hesterly, W. J., and Borgatti, S. P. "A General Theory of Network Governance: Exchange Conditions and Social Mechanisms." *Academy of Management Review,* 1997, *22*(4), 911–945.

Kotter, J. P. *Leading Change.* Boston: Harvard Business School Press, 1996.

Portes, A. "Social Capital: Its Origins and Applications in Modern Sociology." *Annual Review of Sociology,* 1998, *24,* 1–24.

Todeva, E., and Knoke, D. "Strategic Alliances and Models of Collaboration." *Management Decision,* 2005, *43*(1), 123–148.

Weick, K. "Leadership as the Legitimation of Doubt." In W. Bennis, G. M. Spreitzer, and T. G. Cummings (eds.), *The Future of Leadership: Today's Top Leadership Thinkers Speak to Tomorrow's Leaders.* San Francisco: Jossey-Bass, 2001.

C. CASEY OZAKI is a graduate research assistant in the Higher, Adult and Lifelong Education Doctoral Program in the College of Education at Michigan State University.

MARILYN J. AMEY is professor and chair of the Department of Educational Administration at Michigan State University.

JESSE S. WATSON is a graduate research assistant in the Higher, Adult and Lifelong Education Doctoral Program in the College of Education at Michigan State University.

INDEX

Academic standards, dual-enrollment programs and, 72

Accountability, educational partnerships and, 1

Adizes, I., 79

Administration of Justice department (ELAC)–community partnership (case study): awards received and, 35; best practices and, 35–38; certificate/degree programs and, 31–33; community partners and, 31; conclusion, 38–39; department description and, 30–35; education/training promise of, 29, 38; establishing diverse community partners and, 36–37; faculty and, 31; identifying mission/culture and, 35–36; leveraging resources and, 37–38; mission and, 30; reasons for success of, 35, 38; setting of, 30; student club and, 34; students and, 33; treating students as partners and, 37

Adult basic education programs (ABE), 94

Alliances, definition of, 18. See also Connected Campuses of Technology (case study)

American Association of Community and Junior Colleges (AACJC), 94, 97

Amey, M. J., 8, 9, 11

Anderson, E. T., 45

Augustine, C., 95

Bailey, T. R., 70

Baldridge, J. W., 25

Barnett, E., 100

Basu, O. N., 25

Batley, T. R., 70

Baum, H., 45

Baus, F., 7

Bell, K. S., 6, 8

Bernal, H., 46

Boham, K. A., 5

Borgatri, S. P., 106

Bradley, R. T., 93

Bragg, D. D., 5, 8, 53, 100

Brandon, P., 79

Bridges, W., 80–83, 89

Brokers: community colleges as, 10; partnerships and, 55, 110

Brown, D. F., 8, 9, 41

Brumbach, M. A., 51, 53, 55, 59

Bryk, A. S., 109

Campbell, A., 69

Capital: definition of, 49; partnership and, 49. See also Organizational capital; Social capital

Carducci, R., 35, 36

Carl D. Perkins Career and Technical Education Improvement Act of 2006, 96–97

Carnevale, A. P., 76

Carrier, S. M., 51, 53, 55, 59

Champions (initiators), of partnerships: definition of, 11; framing of partnership by, 11, 107; partnership formation and, 7, 106–108; role of, 7–8, 11; social capital of, 11–12; types of, 7

Chin, P., 6, 8

Chung, S., 110

Cohen, D. S., 6, 8, 9, 65, 67

Coleman, J. S., 10, 49, 54, 108, 109

Collaboration: as continuing trend, 17; definitions of, 6–7, 94–95; differing views of, 18; environment and, 94, 100; factors in success of, 17–18; factors influencing successful, 94, 100; as logical approach to needs, 7; membership and, 94, 100–101; model of interdisciplinary, 8–9; problem-solving strategies and, 19; process and structure and, 94, 101; purpose and, 94, 101; resources and, 94, 101; social presence and, 84; successful, and federal policy, 100–101; three-phase model of, 19; transformative ability of, 7. See also Community colleges, as collaborative organizations; Partnerships; Relationships

Collaborative advantage, in partnerships, 42

College and Careers Transition Initiative (CCTI), 97

College education, and economic development, 69

Communication: collaboration and, 94, 101; dual-enrollment programs and, 100; partnerships and, 45. See also

Language, communication, and context, in educational partnership (case study)

Community College P–16 Accelerated Learning Opportunity grant programs, 99–100

Community colleges: broker role of, 6; education/training promise of, 29, 38; as intermediary among educational institutions, 1. *See also* Community colleges, as collaborative organizations; Dual-enrollment programs; *and by individual community college partnerships*

Community colleges, as collaborative organizations: ACJC forums and, 94; access and, 94–95; Carl D. Perkins Career and Technical Education Improvement Act and, 96–97; Community College P–16 Accelerated Learning Opportunity grant programs and, 99–100; federal policy and practice for, 95–98; Illinois Articulation Initiative and, 98–99, 101; motivations of, 95; resource sharing and, 94–95; spectrum of roles of, 95; state policy and practice for, 98–100; types of extended services of, 94; values of, 94; Workforce Investment Act and, 95–96, 101. *See also* Administration of Justice department (ELAC)–community partnership (case study)

Conley, V. M., 73

Connected Campuses of Technology (case study): achieving consensus and, 61; central vs. local decision making and, 63–64; challenges to, 61–64; champions and, 68; context of, 59–60; descriptions of partners and, 60–64; divisiveness within, 62; faculty resistance and, 61–63; as fear driven, 62; financial challenges and, 59–60; formalization of consortium and, 60; funding incentives and, 60, 66; goals of, 59–60; individualism vs. centralization, 63–64; informal alliance and, 60; lack of sustainability and, 66–67; leadership changes and, 59–60; leadership in, 63, 65–66, 68; lessons learned and, 67–68; mandatory nature of, 61, 65; need for clear objectives and, 67; outcomes of, 66–67; power differentials in, 61, 63; relationship tensions in, 63–66; resource sharing

and, 59; setting and, 60; specialization issues and, 66; as successful, 66–67; unclear mission and, 62–63

Consortia, educational, 7. *See also* Partnerships

Context: communication/language and, 43, 46; factors involved in, 7; informal/formal relationships and, 7; partnership formation and, 7. *See also* Language, communication, and context, in educational partnership (case study)

Cooper, J., 79

Creamer, J. S., 10

Criminal justice education. *See* Administration of Justice (AL) department (East Los Angeles College)–community partnership (case study)

Crowther, J., 41

Curtis, D. V., 25

Density, of relationships, 109

Dirsmith, M. W., 25

Distance learning, and partnerships, 6

Distrust, in partnerships, 45

Donovan, R. A., 25

Dougan, C. P., 70

Dual-enrollment programs: alignment of academic standards and, 72; benefits to students of, 76; characteristics of successful, 75–76; collaborative activities and, 99–100; college preparation process and, 74–75; Community College P–16 Accelerated Learning Opportunity grant programs and, 99–100; coordination and, 73; ensuring faculty standards and, 72–73; evaluation and, 75; financial considerations and, 74; goals of, 69; importance of flexibility and, 75; importance of goals/motivation and, 75–76; increasing human capital through, 69, 76; issues of conflict in, 70; issues surrounding, 100; need for clear communication in, 100; need for clear information about, 100; need for strategic management in, 100; need for strong leadership in, 100; policy considerations and, 73–74; policy setting for, 69–70; political considerations and, 74; reasons for, 70; strategic planning need for, 71–72; student support considerations and, 74; teacher-student relationship and, 75.

See also High school–community college dual-enrollment partnership (case study)

East Lost Angeles College (ELAC), 29–38. *See also* Administration of Justice department (ELAC)–community partnership (case study)
Ecker, G. P., 25
Eckerman, W. C., 76
Eddy, P. L., 8, 9, 68
Education Commission of the States, 69
Educational partnerships *See* Partnerships
ELAC. *See* East Los Angeles College; Administration of Justice department (ELAC)–community partnership (case study)
"ELAC's F.I.R.E. Academy Preps Future Fire Fighters," 33
Engineering university–community college partnership (case study): background, 20; benefits to employers of, 21; benefits to institutions of, 21; celebrating milestones and, 23–24; challenges of, 25; descriptions of institutions, 21; external perspective of faculty, 26–27; faculty resistance and, 22–23, 25, 27; implications, 25–26; importance of working together and, 23–24, 26; incentives for partnership and, 20, 26; tasks of partnership and, 19–20, 25; mission and, 21; offering incentives and, 27; partnering process and, 22–24; personnel and, 22; pioneering metaphor and, 19, 27; power of faculty and, 25; procedural autonomy and, 23, 25; recommendations, 26–27; role of champion in, 22, 24, 26; setting of, 20; steps in, 22; transfer and diffusion and, 24
Environment, collaboration and, 94, 100. *See also* Context
Essex, N. L., 7
Evolutionary model, of partnerships, 8

Faculty standards, dual-enrollment programs and, 72–73
Fairhurst, G. T., 9, 68
Fermin, B. J., 70
Fine, G. A., 18, 19, 25
Fisher, J. L., 65, 68
Flynn, R. B., 7, 9, 10, 59
Forney, W., 74

Framing: language issues and, 45; of partnerships, 8, 11; partnership sustainability and, 11; refining multiple interpretations and, 8
Fraser, N., 45
Fry, R. A., 69
Fullan, M., 6, 8, 9

Gardner, D., 100
General educational development (GED) test, 94
Gershwin, M. C., 96
Granovetter, M., 11
Gray, B., 6, 7, 9, 24, 25, 27, 93, 110
Group membership: role of language/context and, 43, 46; role of, in partnerships, 42, 46
Grubb, W. N., 94
Gupta, P. P., 19

Harrell, P., 74
Hesterly, W. J., 106
High school–community college dual-enrollment partnership (case study): alignment of academic standards and, 72; assessment testing and, 71; background on, 69–70; college community resistance to, 71; conclusion, 75–76; coordination and, 73; ensuring faculty standards and, 72–73; evaluation and, 70–71, 75; financial considerations and, 74; origins of, 70; policy considerations and, 73–74; political considerations and, 74; reorganization of, 71; setting of, 70; student responsibilities and, 71; student support considerations and, 74; teacher-student relationship and, 75. *See also* Dual-enrollment programs
High school–community college–university partnership (case study): capital and, 49; context of, 50–51, 55; decision making and, 53–55; definition of terms and, 49–50; description of partners and, 51–53; goals of, 53, 55; motivators and, 53; partner interactions/interrelationships and, 53–55; partner networking and, 53–55; partner positionality and, 53–55; partners as brokers and, 55; partnership and, 49; setting of, 50; sharing facilities and, 50, 55; social capital and, 53–54; transformative effects of, 49; vision/mission of, 50, 52–55

Himmelman, A. T., 93
Hughes, K. L., 70
Hull, D., 96
Hutchinson, N. L., 6, 8
Huxham, C., 42, 43, 46

Ignash, J., 99
Illinois Articulation Initiative (IAI), 98–99, 101
IMED. *See* Interdisciplinary Master's in Education program (UH; case study)
Innovation: Kanter's tasks of, 19–20, 25; organizational model of, 19–20; problem solving and, 19
Interdisciplinary collaboration model, 8–9. *See also* Collaboration
Interdisciplinary Master's in Education program (UH; case study): closing-in stage of, 83; collaboration and, 84; community college–university partnerships and, 81, 89; competition and, 89; conclusions, 89; curriculum design in, 82; dreaming phase of, 81; dying stage of, 83; ecological perspective on, 84, 89; faculty changes and, 83; getting organized stage of, 82; impressionistic tales of, 85–89; institutionalization stage of, 83; interactive TV and, 81–82; launching phase of, 82; life-cycle metaphor and, 79–80, 89; making-it stage of, 83; organizational renewal efforts and, 83; political pressures and, 83–84; program description and, 80–81; purpose of, 80; social presence in, 84; theoretical frameworks and, 79–80; UH College of Education and, 81

Jackson, K. L., 5
Jones, C.,106

Kale, P., 49
Kanter, R. M., 19, 20, 24
Karp, M. M., 70
Keener, B. J., 51, 53, 55
Keener, J. L., 59
Kelly, K. F., 98, 99
Kim, J., 100
Kirst, M. E., 72
Kisker, C. B., 35, 36
Kleinman, N. S., 72
Knoke, D., 109
Kogan, D., 96
Kotter, J. P., 6, 8, 9, 65, 67, 109
Krueger, C., 69, 72, 74

Lach, I. J., 98, 99
Language, communication, and context, in educational partnership (case study): allowing for differential organizational cultures and, 46; barriers to, 41; conflict about grassroots involvement and, 43; conflict about resources and, 44–45; conflict due to language and, 43–44; conflict resolution and, 45–46; discussion, 45–46; distrust and, 45; establishing open communication and, 46; formation process and, 42–43; group membership and, 42, 46; importance of framing and, 45; involvement vs. empowerment and, 43; looking for collaborative advantages and, 46; member roles and, 41; process description, 42–43; purpose and, 41; recommendations, 46; role of language/context and, 43, 46; setting of, 42
Lattuca, L, 9
Leadership: of consortia, 7; need for, in alliances, 65–66, 68. *See also* Champions (initiators), of partnerships
League for Innovation in the Community College, 94, 96–97
Lee, K., 110
Leong, P., 84
Leslie, D. W., 73
Lindberg, M., 79
Location, social capital and, 109
Los Angeles Community College District, 30

McCord, R. S., 5, 6, 55
McDonough, P. M., 74
McFarlane, J. M., 45
Makela, J. P., 100
Martin, J., 18
Mattessich, P. W., 94, 100
Meaders, S. J., 51, 53, 55, 59
Membership, and collaboration, 94, 100–101
Mintzberg, H., 25
Monsey, B. R., 94, 100
Morgan, G., 7, 11, 68, 79, 84
Motivation, partnerships and, 10–11
Multidimensional model of partnership: antecedents of, 9–10, 106; application of, to case studies, 105–108; champions and, 11–12, 106–108; context and, 10; development process of, 11–12; diagram of, *10*; feedback and, 11, 106–107; foundational questions

for, 9; framing and, 11; interdisciplinary collaboration and, 9, 109; motivation and, 10–11; negotiated order theory and, 9; organizational capital and, 11; partnership projections and, 11; policy suggestions and, 111–112; power base and, 11; questions regarding sustainability and, 12; relationships and, 10–11; research themes and, 6–8; sense-making theory and, 9; social and organizational capital and, 110–112; theoretical frameworks and, 9

Munby, H., 6, 8

Negotiated order theory, 9, 18–19, 25
Negotiation: negotiated order theory and, 9, 18–19, 25; process-oriented approach to, 19, 25; steps in, 19

Office of Vocational and Adult Education, 97
O'Hara, P., 11
Organizational capital: formal vs. informal, 109; partnership formation and, 11, 109, 111–113; power base and, 111
Organizational life cycle, 79–80
Organizations: ecological perspective on, 84; life-cycle approach to, 79–80; subsystems of, 84; technology issues and, 82, 84

Partnership formation: champions and, 7–8, 11, 106–107, 111–112; community college as broker and, 6; defining context and, 7; determining the "glue" in, 6, 112; evolution from informal to formal in, 110; evolutionary model of, 8; feedback and, 7, 106–107, 111–112; organizational capital and, 109, 111–113; personal relationships and, 6–7; power base of, 8; process issues and, 7–8; reasons for joining and, 6–7; social capital and, 108–109, 112–113; student learning and, 8; trustworthiness and, 108–111
Partnerships: accountability and, 1; brokers and, 6, 55; capital and, 49; Carl D. Perkins Career and Technical Education Improvement Act and, 96–97; clear objectives in, 67; collaborative advantage and, 42; College and Careers Transition Initiative and, 97; communication and, 45; Community College P–16 Accelerated Learning Opportunity grant programs and, 99–100; consortia and, 7; distance learning and, 6; distrust and, 45; dynamic nature of, 53; elements of successful, 41; failures of, 1–2; federal policy and practice for, 95–98; financial rewards for, 5; framing and, 8, 11; goal setting and, 12; group membership and, 42, 46; Illinois Articulation Initiative and, 98–99, 101; importance of mission in, 35; institutional benefits of, 5; involvement vs. empowerment and, 43; lack of research on, 5; as living systems, 7; motivation and, 10–11; negotiated order theory and, 9, 18–19; organizational capital and, 11; pioneering metaphor and, 19, 27; power issues and, 9, 11, 109; reasons for increase in, 5; relationships and, 6–7, 11; resource sharing and, 59; sense-making theory and, 9; sharing facilities and, 1, 5–6; short-term wins and, 67; state policy and practice for, 98–100; sustainability of, 8, 12; terminology and, 13; themes of, 6–8; Workforce Investment Act and, 95–96, 101. *See also* Administration of Justice department (ELAC)–community partnership (case study); Champions (initiators), of partnerships; Collaboration; Connected Campuses of Technology (case study); Engineering university–community college partnership (case study); High school–community college–university partnership (case study); Language, communication, and context, in educational partnership (case study); Multidimensional model of partnership; Partnership formation; Relationships; Strategic

Perlmutter, H., 49
Portes, A., 108
Power base, in partnerships, 8, 9, 11, 13, 109
Prins, E., 45
Problem solving: individualism vs. interdependence and, 19; collaboration and, 19; dynamic wholeness model and, 19; innovation and, 19–20; negotiated order theory and, 18–19; process-oriented approach to, 19
Process and structure, and collaboration, 94, 101
Purpose, collaboration and, 94, 101

Ramsbottom, C. A., 7
Rasch, E., 99
Reciprocity, social capital and, 108
Reid, K., 46
Relationships: density of, 109; formal and informal, in collaboration, 6–7; multidimensional partnership model and, 11; personal, in partnerships, 6–7; social capital and, 108; trustworthiness and, 108–109
Rendon, L., 75
Resources, and collaboration, 94, 101
Riley, G. L., 25
Roberts, N. C., 93
Rosevear, S., 95
Russell, J. F., 7, 9, 10, 59
Russman, M. A., 96

Sack, J., 98, 99
Samels, J. E., 18
Sarr, R. A., 9, 68
Schaier-Peleg, B., 25
Schneider, B. L., 109
Schockley, D., 5
Schwartz, R. B., 96
Sense-making theory, 9
Shellman, J., 46
Singh, H., 49, 110
Sink, D. W., 6
Social capital: of champions, 11–12, 106–108, 111; definition of, 49, 108; location and, 109; partnership formation and, 108–109, 112–113; reciprocity and, 108; relationships and, 108; time sensitivity and, 109; trustworthiness and, 108, 110
Social presence, technology and, 84
Statewide community college partnerships. See Connected Campuses of Technology (case study)

Strategic partnerships: definition of, 18. See also Engineering university–community college partnership (case study), Partnerships
Strauss, A., 9, 25, 65

Tett, L., 41, 43
Three-phase model of collaboration, 19
Time sensitivity, social capital and, 109
Tinto, V., 74
Todeva, E., 109
Trustworthiness: relational, 108–109; social capital and, 108, 110; sustainability and, 111

UH. See Interdisciplinary Master's in Education program (UH; case study); University of Hawai'i College of Education
University of Hawai'i (UH), College of Education, 81. Interdisciplinary Master's in Education program (UH; case study)
U.S. Department of Labor, 95
U.S. Department of Education, 95

Van Maanen, J., 79
Vangen, S., 42, 43, 46
Vargas, J., 99
Villadsen, A. W., 51, 53, 55, 59

Warford, L. J., 96, 97
Watson, L. W., 6, 7, 9, 53, 55
Weick, K. E., 8, 9, 55, 66, 109
Wilbur, S., 18, 24, 26
Wolverton, M., 65
Workforce Investment Act (WIA) of 1998, 95–96, 101

CC138 **International Reform Efforts and Challenges in Community Colleges**
Edward J. Valeau, Rosalind Latiner Raby
In the post–September 11 era, the effects of globalization are acute and far-reaching. One consequence has been increased recognition that colleges should produce internationally literate graduates who can understand the complexities of our modern world. This volume discusses the role international education plays in developing those graduates and sets the stage for future efforts to make international education an institutionalized and central component of the community college.
ISBN: 978-04701-76887

CC137 **Rural Community Colleges: Teaching, Learning, and Leading in the Heartland**
Pamela L. Eddy, John P. Murray
Funding, faculty and leadership retirements, and shifts in the local economy are all pressing challenges for rural colleges. Expanding partnerships and collaborations, growing future leaders, and lobbying for recognition of the rural resource differential in policy decisions are key for rural campuses. Furthermore, the similarities between large rural institutions and suburban institutions present a nexus for opportunities to share information on best practices and provide a basis for collaboration. This volume identifies issues rural leaders will likely encounter on their campuses and provides a set of tools and strategies to address those issues.
ISBN: 978-07879-97205

CC136 **Community College Missions in the 21st Century**
Barbara K. Townsend, Kevin J. Dougherty
Authors examine both long-standing and emerging societal and functional missions of community colleges. Are traditional missions still relevant? Should the focus be postsecondary education for students who might not otherwise obtain it, or the needs of the local community including business and industry? Providing transfer education? Workforce training and continuing education? This volume's chapters will stimulate thinking and discussion among policy-makers, leaders, scholars, and educators.
ISBN: 0-7879-9575-4

CC135 **Pathways To and From the Community College**
Debra D. Bragg, Elisabeth A. Barnett
Examines local, state, and federal programs to help underserved students enter and succeed in college. Focuses on "academic pathways," boundary-spanning curricula, instructional strategies, and organizational structures to link high schools with two- and four-year colleges. The academic pathways support students during transitions and can be alternate routes to educational attainment. Topics include dual enrollment, dual credit, early and middle college high schools, plus career and technical education pathways and emerging models.
ISBN: 0-7879-9422-7

CC134   **Benchmarking: An Essential Tool for Assessment, Improvement, and
         Accountability**
         Jeffrey A. Seybert
         Comparing your institution's performance to that of its peers is a critical part
         of assessing institutional effectiveness and student learning outcomes. Two-
         year colleges now have access to national data collection and reporting con-
         sortia to identify and benchmark with peer schools. This volume describes
         the costs and benefits of benchmarking, the newly available community
         college data, and how your institution can use it for assessment and
         improvement.
         ISBN: 0-7879-8758-1

CC133   **Latino Educational Opportunity**
         Catherine L. Horn, Stella M. Flores, Gary Orfield
         Latinos enroll at community colleges at rates higher than any other racial
         or ethnic group. Many factors influence Latino education—immigration
         policy, language, academic opportunity, family—and, despite research, the
         influence of these factors remains confounding. This issue explains the ways
         and extent to which community colleges can provide Latino students with
         access and opportunity.
         ISBN: 0-7879-8624-0

CC132   **Sustaining Financial Support for Community Colleges**
         Stephen G. Katsinas, James C. Palmer
         Describes institutional approaches for securing adequate funding in an era of
         recurrent recessions, legislator reluctance to raise taxes, and intense
         competition for scarce resources. Chapter authors give guidelines for
         fundraising, corporate partnerships, grants for workforce development, mill
         levy elections, realigning budget priorities, and the key skills that today's
         community college presidents need.
         ISBN: 0-7879-8364-0

CC131   **Community College Student Affairs: What Really Matters**
         Steven R. Helfgot, Marguerite M. Culp
         Uses the results of a national survey to identify the major challenges and
         opportunities for student affairs practitioners in community colleges, and
         describes the most effective strategies for meeting challenges. Chapters
         discuss core values, cultures of evidence, faculty partnerships, career
         counseling, and support for underrepresented populations, plus assessment
         tools and best practices in student affairs.
         ISBN: 0-7879-8332-2

CC130   **Critical Thinking: Unfinished Business**
         Christine M. McMahon
         With a few exceptions, critical thinking is not being effectively taught or
         even correctly understood in higher education. This volume advocates for
         professional development in critical thinking to engage all members of the
         campus community. It presents blueprints for such development, plus
         practical case studies from campuses already doing it. Also covers classroom
         assignments, solutions to resistance, and program assessment.
         ISBN: 0-7879-8185-0

CC129   **Responding to the Challenges of Developmental Education**
         Carol A. Kozeracki
         Approximately 40 percent of incoming community college students enroll in
         developmental math, English, or reading courses. Despite the availability of
         popular models for teaching these classes, community colleges continue to

struggle with effectively educating underprepared students, who have a wide variety of backgrounds. This volume discusses the dangers of isolating developmental education from the broader college; provides examples of successful programs; offers recommendations adaptable to different campuses; and identifies areas for future research.

ISBN: 0-7879-8050-1

CC128   **From Distance Education to E-Learning: Lessons Along the Way**
Beverly L. Bower, Kimberly P. Hardy
Correspondence, telecourses, and now e-learning: distance education continues to grow and change. This volume's authors examine what community colleges must do to make distance education successful, including meeting technology challenges, containing costs, developing campuswide systems, teaching effectively, balancing faculty workloads, managing student services, and redesigning courses for online learning. Includes case studies from colleges, plus state and regional policy perspectives.

ISBN: 0-7879-7927-9

CC127   **Serving Minority Populations**
Berta Vigil Laden
Focuses on how colleges with emerging majority enrollments of African American, Hispanic, American Indian, Asian American and Pacific Islander, and other ethnically diverse students are responding to the needs— academic, financial, and cultural   of their increasingly diverse student populations. Discusses partnerships with universities, businesses, foundations, and professional associations that can increase access, retention, and overall academic success for students of color. Covers best practices from Minority-Serving Institutions, and offers examples for mainstream community colleges.

ISBN: 0-7879-7790-X

CC126   **Developing and Implementing Assessment of Student Learning Outcomes**
Andreea M. Serban, Jack Friedlander
Colleges are under increasing pressure to produce evidence of student learning, but most assessment research focuses on four-year colleges. This volume is designed for practitioners looking for models that community colleges can apply to measuring student learning outcomes at the classroom, course, program, and institutional levels to satisfy legislative and accreditation requirements.

ISBN: 0-7879-7687-3

CC125   **Legal Issues in the Community College**
Robert C. Cloud
Community colleges must be prepared for lawsuits, federal statutes, court rulings, union negotiations, and other legal issues that could affect institutional stability and effectiveness. This volume provides leaders with information about board relations, tenure and employment, student rights and safety, disability law, risk management, copyright and technology issues, and more.

ISBN: 0-7879-7482-X

NEW DIRECTIONS FOR COMMUNITY COLLEGES
Order Form
SUBSCRIPTIONS AND SINGLE ISSUES

DISCOUNTED BACK ISSUES:

Use this form to receive **20% off** all back issues of New Directions for
Community Colleges. All single issues are priced at **$23.20** (normally $29.00).

TITLE	ISSUE NO.	ISBN

Call 888-378-2537 or see mailing instructions below. When calling, mention the
promotional code JB7ND to receive your discount.

SUBSCRIPTIONS: *(1 year, 4 issues)*

☐ New Order   ☐ Renewal

U.S.	☐ Individual: $80	☐ Institutional: $195
Canada/Mexico	☐ Individual: $80	☐ Institutional: $235
All Others	☐ Individual: $104	☐ Institutional: $269

Call 888-378-2537 or see mailing and pricing instructions below. Online
subscriptions are available at www.interscience.wiley.com.

Copy or detach page and send to:
**John Wiley & Sons, Journals Dept, 5th Floor
989 Market Street, San Francisco, CA 94103-1741**

Order Form can also be faxed to: 888-481-2665

Issue/Subscription Amount: $ _____	**SHIPPING CHARGES:**
Shipping Amount: $ _____	SURFACE Domestic Canadian
(for single issues only—subscription prices include shipping)	First Item $5.00 $6.00
Total Amount: $ _____	Each Add'l Item $3.00 $1.50

(No sales tax for U.S. subscriptions. Canadian residents, add GST for subscription orders. Individual rate subscriptions
must be paid by personal check or credit card. Individual rate subscriptions may not be resold as library copies.)

☐ Payment enclosed (U.S. check or money order only. All payments must be in U.S. dollars.)

☐ VISA   ☐ MC   ☐ Amex # _____ Exp. Date _____

Card Holder Name _____ Card Issue # _____

Signature _____ Day Phone _____

☐ Bill Me (U.S. institutional orders only. Purchase order required.)

Purchase order # _____
Federal Tax ID13559302   GST 89102 8052

Name _____

Address _____

Phone _____ E-mail _____

JB7ND